PLAYING HARDBALL WITH SOFT SKILLS

PLAYING HARDBALL WITH SOFT SKILLS

How to Prosper with Non-Technical
Skills in a High-Tech World

Steven J. Bennett

BANTAM BOOKS
TORONTO · NEW YORK · LONDON · SYDNEY · AUCKLAND

PLAYING HARDBALL WITH SOFT SKILLS
A Bantam Book / February 1986

Book Design by Nicola Mazzella

Library of Congress Cataloging-in-Publication Data

Bennett, Steven J.
  Playing hardball with soft skills.

  Bibliography: p. 193
  Includes index.
  1. New business enterprises.   2. Entrepreneur.
3. Success in business.   I. Title.
HD62.5.B46   1986   650.1   85-47796
ISBN 0–553–34233–9

Published simultaneously in the United States and Canada

*Bantam Books are published by Bantam Books, Inc. Its trade-
mark, consisting of the words "Bantam Books" and the por-
trayal of a rooster, is Registered in U.S. Patent and Trademark
Office and in other countries. Marca Registrada. Bantam
Books, Inc., 666 Fifth Avenue, New York, New York 10103.*

PRINTED IN THE UNITED STATES OF AMERICA

O   0 9 8 7 6 5 4 3 2 1

To my parents,
Albert and Marilyn, who allowed me
to follow my nose.

ACKNOWLEDGMENTS

The ideas in this book germinated for almost a decade. But as book writing often goes, actually putting it together happened in what seems like the blink of an eye. That required a great deal of help from other people, to whom I'm deeply indebted for their energy, time, and all-out effort.

Many thanks go to my literary agent, friend, and fellow Soft-Skilled Entrepreneur, H. Michael Snell, whose incisive comments and criticisms gave my manuscript much-needed shape and direction. Throughout the writing process, Mike patiently guided me through the joys and pains of constructing a book. My editor, Peter Guzzardi, believed in the book from the beginning, and his enthusiastic suggestions always made it better and more useful.

I also owe a great debt to two friends and colleagues, Charlie Levin and Peter Kinder, who steadfastly listened to crazy ideas and injected a measure of reality at all hours of the day and night. The book would not have been possible without the help of Lisa Miller, researcher and interviewer *par excellence*. Someday she'll make the list of the 100 Greatest Soft-Skilled Entrepreneurs. I'd also like to thank Alissa Stern, Eve Kahn, Dianne Ring, and Patrice Hall for their research contributions; Bruce Sunstein and Jan Williams for their comments on the manuscript; Jeff Strauss, the only living disciple of Master Hui, for his suggested refinements; and Kathryn Nettles for superbly coordinating a lot of messy details.

Last, but never least, my most heartfelt thanks go to my wife, Ruth, who supported my obsession despite the many evenings and weekends my work on the manuscript kept us apart.

CONTENTS

INTRODUCTION: NOTES FROM A SURVIVOR OF THE BABY BOOM

WHEN THE GOOD SHIP WENT DOWN

Nineteen-seventy-three was a good year for some California chardonnay and cabernet wines. It was a horrible year for just about everything else. What with the oil embargo, the recession, the aftermath of Vietnam, and the unfolding of Watergate, most Americans had something to worry about. Those in academia had the best reasons for keeping a good supply of Pepto Bismol on hand: in April 1973 the Carnegie Commission on Higher Education released a bombshell report entitled *College Graduates and Jobs: Adjusting to a New Labor Market Situation.* It should have been called "The Road to Hell Is Paved with Ph.D.'s." According to the Commission's projections, by the mid-1980's anywhere from 40,000 to 80,000 people would win doctoral sheepskins in everything from entomology to Mesopotamian history. Unfortunately, the number of new Ph.D.'s required for academic teaching in the mid-1980's would have plunged to zero. To make matters worse, the Commission speculated that no more than 50 percent of the excess Ph.D.'s could find jobs in government or industry. That would leave 20,000 to 40,000 losers beating a path to the end of the unemployment line.

Nevertheless, undaunted by those dire predictions and consumed by my dream of becoming a professional scholar, in the fall of 1973 I entered a graduate program in Chinese studies.

I would certainly land a job; not only was I getting a degree from Harvard, but I was tackling a topic that only a handful of scholars in the world knew anything about: the history of Far Eastern science. Surely, even in the worst of times there would be a tenured slot for someone who knew the finer points of Chinese astronomy, alchemy, and medicine.

To help ensure my career, my adviser recommended that I map an uncharted area, one that would make me a priceless addition to any East Asian Studies department. Soon I found myself exploring the mysterious and little-known practice of "geomancy," the two-thousand-year-old science of situating residences for the living and tombs for the dead.

Within a year and a half I had excavated and pored through stacks of geomancy texts buried in the bowels of Harvard's Asiatic library and had cornered the market on the subject. I learned where to place a house when a stream slices through a mountain, what land forms to look for when orienting a tomb, and how to keep the cosmic energy in one site from flowing into another.

The more I carved out my niche, the more I became convinced that I'd entered the fast lane to scholastic stardom. Then, at the end of my second year, unemployment horror stories became more popular than speculation about President Ford's ability to chew gum and walk at the same time. Those who kept a close ear to the academic grapevines reported that as many as two hundred qualified people were applying for each teaching position in East Asian studies. Many of the candidates had five or more years of teaching experience and had authored one or two books. Even people from Harvard were having trouble. *Even people from Harvard?*

By 1976 the prospects for a career teaching Chinese culture looked grim at best. And the problem wasn't just in the field of East Asian studies; like America's automobiles, the entire academic enterprise seemed to have run out of gas. In reality, society had just run out of space for Baby Boomers who didn't make any tangible contribution to the Gross National Product. As a result, graduate students of my era had unwittingly become members of a new caste of unemployables, educated to the highest standards, but without a shred of preparation for the real world.

Many of us fled, packing up our degrees and bailing out of higher education altogether. (Those diehards who chose to hide

out in the library stacks have probably collected as much dust as
the geomancy texts I left behind in the basement.) Some of my
peers registered for undergraduate science courses and then went
on to medical school. Others applied to law school. Still others
enrolled in business school or went to work for the government.
And some never collected the pieces of their shattered dreams;
they're now holding the pickles and lettuce at Burger King.

Had I slaved all those years only to end up plugging hernias,
drafting estate forms, finding Third World markets for bras-
sieres, helping Uncle Sam waste more trees on useless memos, or
draining the grease from french-fry baskets? Or was it possible
that I could parlay a master's degree in Chinese Studies into
something lucrative as well as satisfying?

DOWN SO LOW, I HAD TO REACH UP
TO TIE MY SHOES

I began my quest for the holy paycheck by pounding the turf
that seemed most fallow for a scholarly soul like myself: publishing houses, educational research outfits, public television, and
other quasi-intellectual organizations. Surely, some insightful
employer would pay dearly for my knowledge of ancient Chinese
science.

But no one did. Each prospective employer found me interesting but useless. Not even "overqualified," just plain useless! After six months I actually contemplated mental suicide—law
school. Not only was I sick of barely supporting myself with part-
time jobs loading trucks and selling basement waterproofing, but
I couldn't take much more ego battering.

To soothe my hurting pride I conjured up conversations between Master Hui, an all-purpose philosopher-sage who inhab-
ited the inner realm of my imagination, and a disciple named
Shen Ti, my upstart alter ego who often managed to look at the
world in a way that surprised the Master. When Master Hui
quoted an inspiring passage from the *Tao Te Ching*, a mystical
ancient philosophy text that says: "Reversal is the movement of
the Way," Shen Ti interpreted the text to mean: "Once your life
hits the pits, there's only one way it can go—up."

Although I didn't know it at the time, my own life reversal

began during a particularly devastating job interview. The interviewer did a double take at my résumé (which prominently featured my expertise in Chinese science, geomancy, and cosmology) and, suppressing a smile, asked, "You're kidding, right? What the hell could you possibly do for us?" I surprised myself by saying, "I've had valuable training. I've studied things no one else understands. If I can unravel Chinese geomancy, I can master anything you can throw at me!" For a moment he looked thoughtful, seemingly impressed by my answer and chutzpah, but he shook his head and advised, "Go to law school, Steve."

I left feeling frustrated and angry, but with a glimmer of an idea forming in my mind. By God, I probably *could* learn anything, but I'd never get a chance to prove it unless I could bluff my way through the interview game. I immediately overhauled the résumé that had always given away my losing hand. The new version turned some bad cards into trumps: my graduate program became "advanced studies in the history of science and technology"; Chinese geomancy turned into "non-Western environmental engineering"; and my degree in Chinese itself, formally stated on my diploma as "Regional Studies—East Asia," simply became "Regional Studies." No one ever asked me what that meant, and one interviewer assumed I had studied the transfer of technology to the Sun Belt.

My new pitch got me back into the game. People began taking me more seriously, and I dealt myself a couple of small winning hands. One landed me a part-time research assistantship with a clinical psychologist who was studying learning disabilities at a local children's hospital. The other connected me with a film producer who needed archival research for a new series on the history of medicine. Both jobs died of funding starvation after six months, but each left me with a hot new card: now I could claim to have worked for a prestigious medical institution and a prominent science film producer.

Playing my new aces, I won a job as the research coordinator of the Center for Short-Lived Phenomena, an organization that reported on earthquakes, volcanic eruptions, insect infestations, frog wars, raining fish, and environmental disasters such as oil and hazardous waste spills. A year later, after learning how to interview scientists and write technical briefs, I gambled that I could apply such skills to other areas and left the Center to sign on as the director of research at a political advertising and consulting firm. My experience there proved I really could transfer my general skills and abilities to any area, but more important, it gave me the confidence to set out on my own. After all, my employers during the past two years had been people my own age. Why couldn't I become my own boss?

Such thinking led to an ill-fated publishing company that produced the worst bibliography of health books ever compiled, a snazzy "No Nukes Is Good Nukes" T-shirt line (profits from which went to an alternative-energy group), and the first one-way street map of Cambridge—which, it turned out, had a worldwide market of 13. Broke, deeply in debt, and disheartened, my partner (another refugee from the political advertising firm) and I traded the copyright to our map for a hot lunch, then went our separate ways. While he chose the sensible path to medical school, I wandered back to the employment poker table.

Although the collapse of my publishing empire left me somewhat chastened, I soon found my failures actually putting my life into better focus. I began to understand how seemingly unconnected bits and pieces of my experience could fit together into a clear map leading toward my financial and life-style goals. It all depended on how I played my cards. As the song goes, "every hand's a winner, every hand's a loser." So it was that my business flops became "professional experience," ranging from "publication development" and "book production" to "specialty garment production" and "cartographic design." No one ever asked if those projects had turned a profit.

Despite my shaky start as an entrepreneur, the freedom and flexibility of self-employment meant more to me than the security of a weekly paycheck, and I felt confident that I could make a good living if I channeled my energy and experience in the right direction. To emphasize my communication skills, I ordered some stationery that proclaimed me to be a "communications consultant." Before long, that letterhead landed me a consulting job with the federal government writing histories, annual reports, and recruitment brochures for the Peace Corps and other volunteer programs. Given the respectable fee I received for this interesting work, I decided to pursue government consulting for the next few years. That aspiration, however, was cut short when a new administration swept into Washington, slashed the federal volunteer programs, and chased most consultants out of the District.

Back in Cambridge, I ran into an old friend who crowed about the lucrative ghostwriting she'd been doing for physicians and scientists. Assuming that an ex-geomancer would find that line of work a snap, I retooled the old résumé to reflect my science-writing expertise and contacted the local chapter of the American Medical Writers Association. The Association soon led me to an assignment ghostwriting a paper on a subject I couldn't even pronounce. Did I feel intimidated? About as much as I had when I first began unlocking the secrets of Chinese geomancy five years before. But I knew it was just a matter of digging up the right text for teaching myself the smattering of chemistry and physiology I needed to translate the topic into English. Eventually the paper I wrote appeared in a journal, a success that brought similar assignments, more self-teaching, greater confidence, higher rates, and tremendous satisfaction.

Over the next three years I built up a broad base of scientific, technical, and medical knowledge, eventually developing a knack for simplifying complex technical issues for lay people. This talent laid the cornerstone for a business that quickly grew from a one-person writing service to a fully staffed technical publishing and advertising company that now produces everything from laboratory training guides and product brochures to software and computer manuals.

The $250 seed money I planted to start S. J. Bennett & Company, Inc., has sprouted into gross revenues as high as $500,000 a year, more than enough to afford me a life-style I enjoy. I take special satisfaction, though, from the knowledge that despite the numerous shark attacks, whirlpools, and hurricanes I encountered after abandoning a sinking academic ship, my free spirit has guided me to a safe shore. I still have to work hard, and I must learn new skills every day. But I am fulfilling my dream of playing hardball with soft skills.

My own story is not unique. I've met all sorts of people who've bailed out of dead-end jobs to create satisfying and self-supporting niches for themselves. These survivors share two common attributes: they want to achieve financial security without sacrificing life-style goals in the process, and they have backgrounds in literature, history, fine arts, psychology, and other "soft" fields with no obvious value in a world that's becoming more high-tech every day. Yet, despite this "disadvantage," they've achieved success without retraining in some technical discipline. Instead, they've learned to use their existing skills and abilities in new and profitable ways. I call my fellow survivors "Soft-Skilled Entrepreneurs" (SE's), and have learned much from their successes and failures.

WHEN THE GOING GETS TOUGH, THE TOUGH TURN PRO

For some years now I have kept a journal that contains stories about SE's, stunning examples of successful SE projects, detailed notes about important SE techniques, and a number of imaginary conversations between Master Hui (the traditional approach) and Shen Ti (the soft-skilled upstart with an alternative vision). After realizing that my journal could help other soft-skilled people create satisfying livelihoods, I turned it into a manual for surviving the "Techno Age," an era when many people assume that a lack of technical skills condemns them to a low-income life of servitude. This book, which is based on my studies of Soft-Skilled Entrepreneurs, destroys that myth.

Playing Hardball with Soft Skills shows you how to take charge of your life and begin working toward your life-style and financial goals. Unlike how-to-get-hired books, which help you prepare for job roles and job markets, *Playing Hardball* encourages you to become your own boss, even if you choose to do so within an existing company. Whether you strike out on your own or strike back at the system from within, you'll find the tactics in this book invaluable to your cause.

Those people who don't want to sacrifice the security of a regular paycheck and benefits can adopt SE techniques to build "companies within companies," seizing opportunities to grow and advance within a company by creating a new division, a new system, or a new way of doing things. Whatever your preference, you'll learn a proven method for creating successful projects tailored to your own needs and goals, be they ones you let your current employer finance or ones you start in your own basement.

First you'll learn how to prepare yourself psychologically for success by overcoming self-imposed barriers and limitations. Then you'll see how to identify and make use of abilities and skills you never knew you had. Once you feel comfortable with your new repertoire of capabilities, you'll find out how to put them to good use conceiving and developing projects that can make you master of your financial destiny, without compromising important goals and values.

Throughout the book you'll find conversations between Master Hui and Shen Ti, followed by stories of SE's whose practical experience illustrates the point being made. Examples range from SE's who are content with part-time, home-based enterprises to SE's who have built multimillion-dollar ventures from humble beginnings in their basements. As different and as unusual as the stories may be, each one fits certain patterns that can benefit anyone, regardless of his or her own unique background.

As you learn about the tools you'll need to survive and flourish in the Techno Age, you'll also discover where to find the cutting edge—SE-style opportunities that someone with your special skills can turn into hard cash. Each chapter in this book constitutes a road map of our rapidly changing techno-economy, and covers topics ranging from computers and work-styles to health care and life-styles. You'll find numerous core ideas that can generate lucrative enterprises tailored to your abilities, interests, and resources. It's up to you whether you develop a part-time project in your home, expand your ideas into a financial empire, or let your employer finance your ambition.

WHO CAN PLAY HARDBALL
WITH SOFT SKILLS?

Just about any soft-skilled person can be a winner in the Techno Age. But you're most likely to profit from this book if:

- You hold or are finishing a degree in the arts and humanities and are looking for a way to make a decent living without selling out your values or life-style goals. *Playing Hardball with Soft Skills* will show you a variety of ways to apply your communication and research skills to the business world.

- You have a job or career but are bored with it or sick of it. You want to find a way to better use your skills and abilities within the company or on your own.

- You had a job, but it vanished when your employer went belly-up, the industry you're working in collapsed, or your title simply dissolved with changing times. *Playing Hardball* will show you how to transfer your work experience to a successful new venture.

- You're an undergraduate facing important career decisions. You're not interested in training for one of the conventional professions, but you're not thrilled at the prospect of massaging a cash register either. *Playing Hardball* will help you choose courses that will allow you to exploit the opportunities looming on the horizon. When you've finished school, you'll be well-armed to thrive in the Techno Age.

HOW TO USE THIS BOOK

Depending on your needs and preferences, you can use this book in several ways. You'll benefit most if you read through each chapter, completing all the self-tests and exercises. If you're in a hurry, you can scan the examples of successful SE's and try the exercises that appeal to you. This brief tour will at least give you the gist of what playing hardball with soft skills is all about, and how you can prosper in the Techno Age.

Finally, if you've already mastered basic training, you might use *Playing Hardball* purely as a resource book. The SE Library at the end of the book contains many useful references to books, periodicals, and organizations that can help you start, develop, and maintain specific projects of interest to you.

Whichever way you go, you're bound to have fun. You might get rich. And best of all, you may find yourself enjoying life in the year 2000.

1
TAKING THE TECHNO AGE BY STORM: THE SOFT-SKILLED ENTREPRENEUR

The spring of the year of the horse was warm and serene in the Lu Valley. Master Hui Tzu, renowned philosopher, decided to celebrate the new season by taking his disciples down to the banks of the Yangtze River, where he would begin lecturing on the architecture of the cosmos.

"The river is a cosmos in miniature," Master Hui told his students. "It eternally moves onward, just as the Great Flow of cosmic energy has supported the universe since the beginning of time. Observe the myriad life forms darting about the water— they are like sun and moon and all that exists between heaven and earth. Watch carefully, and you will understand how the cosmos is one great temple."

Everyone gazed into the water until disciple Shen Ti broke the silence by exclaiming, "With all due respect, Master Hui, I cannot agree. Having meditated on the life forms in the river, I can see that the universe actually sits on the back of a great turtle."

The Master stroked his beard thoughtfully, then challenged his disciple, saying, "This is interesting, Shen Ti. But tell me, what lies under the turtle?"

"Oh, you're not going to catch me on that one," Shen Ti exclaimed. "It's turtles all the way down!"

A SEA OF PLENTY

Turtles resting on turtles resting on turtles—that's a good way to think about our economy. Each of us fits into the stack somewhere, and most people wouldn't mind climbing up a shell or two to improve their position. But whether or not you ascend depends largely on how you play the game. You can follow the traditional rules, training for a career and slowly advancing up the pile, or you can follow unconventional rules, creating your own employment situation and taking an express elevator to the top.

In this turbulent Techno Age it makes increasing sense to take the express route. Innovative technologies have spawned new work-styles, life-styles, leisure-styles, and health-styles that in turn offer endless opportunities for creating personal wealth. And the winning stakes have reached an all-time high; more people than ever are now finding it possible to succeed in a way that supports both their monetary goals and their most important life values.

Fortunately, the possibilities for cashing in lie within easy grasp even for those who have no technical training. In fact, the Techno Age may well go down in history as having opened more doors for people with nontechnical backgrounds than for those steeped in computers and electronics. A paradox? Not at all. The demand for technically skilled people will gradually become satisfied, until we have a glut of engineers, programmers, and other hard-core technical types who, like the high-flying aerospace engineers of the sixties, will end up playing electronic games between visits to the unemployment office. But by that time the need for specialized goods and services to help people and businesses cope with the economic and social changes wrought by the new technologies will have mushroomed. Such spin-offs, many of which are best exploited by people who *don't* have technical backgrounds, will continue to multiply long after the initial impact of the technological revolution fades. It will be like watching a meteor plunge into the ocean—the waves will continue to radiate outward even though the rock disappeared long ago. All you have to do is catch a wave to the shore of your choice.

At this very moment, thousands of nontechnical souls are already riding the ripples of the Techno Age, turning their soft skills into hard cash. Many are making money from the computer invasion, which has left in its wake countless opportunities for people with old-fashioned teaching and writing skills. Some are fulfilling an ever-growing need for instruction in basic computing, with consulting services, schools, seminars, and camps aimed at helping neophytes learn what to do once they've uncrated their new toys. These entrepreneurs take advantage of the fact that the more computers invade the workplace and the home, the more people fear being left behind their co-workers, neighbors, and kids. They also know that the business of treating "techno-illnesses" such as computerphobia requires no advanced training, because anyone who knows how to learn can buy or rent a computer and some software, read the manuals, become an expert by trial and error, and then hang out a shingle. More than a few fortunes have been made that way, and the door has just begun to swing open, especially for entrepreneurs who offer training to doctors, dentists, lawyers, architects, and other specialized stragglers in the computer revolution.

Many soft-skilled people focus on computers in education, a blossoming Techno Age trend. The proliferation of educational software has created a tremendous need for people who can help educators sift through the bewildering array of new products and buy the right stuff. And as more school systems install the computers they've begged for, they will require increasing outside help to get the most out of the machines. Who will ride to the rescue? Not computer engineers, but spirited teachers and communicators who see the computer for what it is: a simple tool that anyone can put to productive use.

Some soft-skilled people find they can make $50, $75, even $100 an hour rewriting technical gibberish into plain English. The explosion of new software has been offset by an implosion in the quality of manuals. Smart software developers who now realize that their manuals really do affect sales are emphasizing excellent writing first, technical know-how second. People who can write clearly and effectively will find a wealth of opportunities waiting for them as the software industry matures.

Other Techno Age opportunities have sprung up in the information field. As our economy steadily moves from a manufacturing base to an information base, practically unlimited possibilities have unfolded for making money by selling, compiling, retrieving, and brokering information. Many soft-skilled people can take advantage of this trend by setting up information-retrieval services, pulling down handsome fees to search data bases for marketing, product, regulatory, and other information of use to researchers, professionals, corporations, and institutions. And while information has always been power, in the Techno Age it has also become money in the pocket.

As new technologies affect *how* we do business, they also begin to affect *where* we do business. And there's a growing Techno Age trend to do it in your living room, kitchen, or basement. Not only can someone with a microcomputer and some inexpensive hardware set up an electronic library in his or her home, but also some companies now allow employees to "telecommute," supplying them with computers so they can do their work at home. As "telecommuting" gathers momentum, it will create a demand for people who can provide the resources and tools that support this new work-style.

Not all of the action in the Techno Age directly involves technology's gadgets. In fact, excellent opportunities will arise from a growing countertrend: the more high technology affects our lives, the more we will hunger for nontechnical relief. This "high-tech backlash" has already created new corporate departments, hundreds of cottage businesses, and consulting firms catering to leisure, personal fitness, and other humanistic pursuits. Once computers are humming in all our offices and homes, we'll have more time to worry about things we've always worried about: sex and relationships, money and taxes, birth and children, health and death.

As a result, entrepreneurs will make money in areas like continuing education, "schools without walls," executive training programs, and adult education. As the need for technical knowledge increases, so will the desire for nontechnical courses and programs. Those trained in teaching the humanities and those who have expertise in arts, crafts, and other forms of self-expression stand on the threshold of a golden era.

Similarly, in the area of personal health, soft-skilled people can look forward to new ways of making a living from current trends in nutrition, exercise, and fitness. More and more corporations are lavishing funds on facilities and programs to keep their employees healthy, and individuals are spending record sums on home exercise equipment that used to be found only in health clubs and gyms. This bespeaks the growing number of Techno Age niches for people who can help others take responsibility for their personal well-being.

Leisure-related projects will also flourish in the years to come. Notice how in the midst of the high-tech boom video games fizzled while simple card and board games like Trivial Pursuit and Decipher became blockbusters. At the same time the cultural media have cited new and intense interests in traveling, gardening, gourmet cooking, and other nontechnical activities that make life more satisfying in the Techno Age. The possibilities for soft-skilled people to capitalize on these trends are limited only by the bounds of their imaginations.

Who are the people taking advantage of these Techno Age trends? On one level they're ordinary people, unlikely to succeed in the business world. But on another they've become consummate players of the shell game, attaining their unique financial, life-style, and career goals through unconventional approaches to business. And in doing so they've come to typify a new breed of winner: the Soft-Skilled Entrepreneur (SE).

HORATIO ALGER IN THE 1980'S

Soft-Skilled Entrepreneurs are old-fashioned American heroes, living proof that anyone in this country can make it if he or she applies enough elbow grease to the right cogs. SE's represent all ages, races, and creeds. They hail from the Northeast, the South, the Midwest, the Southwest, the West Coast, and the Northwest. They live in Boston, New York, Chicago, San Francisco, small towns in Vermont, and the corn fields of Iowa. They hold degrees in literature, history, anthropology, fine arts, sociology, psychology, and religion. They've been cabdrivers, writers, teachers, editors, secretaries, lifetime students, bookkeepers, salespeople, and just about anything else one can do for a living. Like you and me, they're very ordinary people with extraordinary drives.

These modern-day Horatio Algers can make a project fly even if they have to start on a shoestring, launching money-making enterprises with nothing but a hot insight, some makeshift letterhead stationery, a borrowed typewriter, and a telephone. Few of them enjoy formal business training or experience, or, for that matter, have any burning desire to swing through the business jungle. Nevertheless, their ideas often pay off handsomely, creating great personal wealth and satisfaction. Profiles of successful Soft-Skilled Entrepreneurs could easily fill this entire book. And as different as their cases may be, each SE is motivated by the same desire to balance financial, life-style, and career goals. Like most people, SE's want to earn as much money as they can. But they don't want to march strictly to the chime of cash registers. Many SE's are equally—and sometimes more— concerned with exercising their creativity and having control over their lives, by choosing *what* they work on; *whom* they work with; *when* they work; and *where* they work.

As Judith Garelick, who holds a Ph.D. in American literature and now works as an independent financial and investment counselor, puts it: "There's a great sense of power in not being dependent on the approval or disapproval of some superior for your career future. Instead, you're dependent on how well you can communicate your abilities and how hard you're willing to work. So you have a much greater degree of control over your own fate."

And Richard Canter, an academic turned builder, agrees that "working for yourself has an important advantage: you can create a business that reflects your way of looking at the world, rather than working at a business where a world view is handed to you on a plate."

SCANNING THE LANDSCAPES
OF OPPORTUNITY

The SE's secret to success is a sixth sense, a kind of radar that zeroes in on moneymaking opportunities invisible to everyone else. This capability, which you'll acquire as you read on, enables SE's to quickly exploit the events and trends that are shaping the Techno Age.

Here's a good example of how the SE's mind works. *The Wall Street Journal* once ran a lead article stating that the major manufacturers of microcomputers are desperately trying to convince the public that home computers are the appliances of the eighties and that no modern household can operate without one. Most readers would:

a) find the idea interesting or amusing;
b) find it appalling;
c) find it silly;
d) accept it as a natural artifact of the computer invasion; or
e) not think anything of it at all.

The Soft-Skilled Entrepreneur, however, would immediately imagine several ways to take advantage of the manufacturers' marketing plight:

1. A small business that organizes "Microware" parties modeled on the successful Tupperware parties. The SE would charge the computer manufacturers a fee for organizing the event and would receive a commission on each machine sold at the gathering.

2. A service that locates and interviews users who *have* made personal computers an indispensable appliance. The information could be sold as market research to the computer manufacturers and could even be developed into an ongoing newsletter.

3. A service that arranges for "Micro Openers"—open houses where home-computer addicts show off their machine expertise to potential buyers. The manufacturers would pay a flat fee for each open house, and the addict would receive a valuable piece of software or equipment from the manufacturer for his or her time.

4. "Micro Mobile," which, like the bookmobiles, takes computers and software into neighborhoods so people can try them out. The software would focus on education, entertainment, and productivity.

5. A new benefit program within a company's personnel department. The program would help employees purchase home computers on which they can perform some important company assignments. Employees receive a good discount, enjoy the personal use of a computer, and might even graduate to the brave new world of telecommuting.

The first four ideas contain several built-in features that make them ideally suited to Soft-Skilled Entrepreneurship: 1) they could be started with whatever funds were available—from $50 to $50,000. The level of capitalization would simply determine how much "sweat equity" that SE had to invest, and how rapidly the enterprise grew; 2) each project idea exploits a newly identified need, too new to be satisfied by conventional means; and, 3) *one could profit from each with almost no prior knowledge of computers!* The fifth idea allows someone currently employed to apply SE tactics within the firm.

Regardless of the project, lack of prior knowledge never thwarts an SE. Not only can SE's operate with whatever resources are available, but they have seldom been formally trained in the fields they come to conquer. Even in such highly specialized areas as brain surgery and nuclear engineering, any soft-skilled person can learn the general concepts and techno lingo, and then use abilities such as organizing people and researching topics to become an overnight "expert."

If this sounds farfetched, think of the infamous case of the "great imposter," Ferdinand Demara, a high-school dropout who masqueraded as at least five distinguished professionals, including a surgeon during the Korean War. Demara, who had never performed surgery, read a number of medical texts and on that basis performed complicated *MASH*-style surgical wonders, saving a number of lives! While it's not advisable to open a home-style surgical shop, you too can become a technical chameleon and perform feats of daring in the Techno Age by living out the credo of the Soft-Skilled Entrepreneur: first, develop the right attitude (Chapter 2); next, cultivate your hidden skills (Chapter 3); then employ the right techniques to create Techno Age opportunities (Chapters 4–7).

QUICK-CHANGE ARTISTS

Because SE's don't feel intimidated by their lack of training or experience in a specific opportunity area, they often undergo what appear to be wild career changes. If you're having any doubts about whether you can really strike out on your own or make a bold move from within, consider these transformations:

- former college instructor Lora Vivilecchia (M.A. Communication Skills) now runs SpeechComm, which shows executives how to write and present effective speeches and enhance their communication abilities.

- former school administrator Alfred Poor (Ph.D. School and Community Relations) now runs SoftIndustries, a consulting firm that helps companies locate computer and software systems that meet their needs.

- former part-time college teacher Peter Van den Noort (B.A. English Literature) now operates the Word Processors' Collective, a placement service for people with professional word processing experience.

- former student Stephanie Anderson (B.A. Spanish/ Creative Writing) stepped out of school into a self-made career as a fitness consultant.

- former executive secretary/translator Cynthia Euske (B.A. French) started Central Penn Translation Services, which specializes in translating American and European technical manuals.

- former junior-college teacher Jane Poston (B.A. Psychology, M.A. English Literature) started a house-sitting service that primarily relies on retirees in the Tucson area. She even wrote a book: *How to Run a House-Sitting Business.*

All of these people—and every other Soft-Skilled Entrepreneur in this book—either grew tired of the status quo or spotted an emerging trend they could capitalize on with their existing talents. Such motivation for change is the key element of SE success stories.

"And what else can you learn from observing the river?"
Master Hui asked Shen Ti.
"When you toss a pebble into the water, everything changes yet nothing changes," the disciple replied as he pitched a small stone from the bank. "See what happens to the water striders as the waves fan out from the stone? Does each ripple overpower them? No, they magically ride in place, barely disturbed by the event. This is the way of the Sage."
Master Hui nodded in approval.

From vacuum tubes to microchips. Robert Florzak of Chicago rode the waves of high-tech change to become computer-competent, and now helps others do the same. An experienced public-relations practitioner and journalist, Florzak has used his communications and reporting skills to leave behind the "Radio Age" in which he was born and become attuned to the silicon era.

When his son chose computers as a career, Florzak found he could no longer understand his offspring spouting about "16- and 32-bit machines, disk-operating systems, modems, and other incomprehensible things." Rather than throw up his hands in despair, he researched computers, took a couple of night courses, and visited computer stores, asking questions until he could understand—and match—his son's jargon bit for byte.

Once he began giving talks and writing articles, Florzak realized that thousands of other people his age were experiencing the same problems he had experienced. As a function of his P.R./ marketing practice, he formed Infomedia Processors based on the microcomputer as the "ultimate communication medium." He then began helping executives overcome their fear of computers by showing how they could be used productively for everything from word processing and financial reports to telecommunications and data-base searches.

Says Florzak: "Computers are everywhere, affecting every kind of business. You certainly can't work in any phase of public communications and hide from them. Unfortunately, lots of middle-age executives shun microcomputers because they're afraid they'll lose status by looking dumb. And they especially seem to resent having a twenty-four-year-old whiz kid come in and tell them how to run their business by technical means they don't fully understand. That's where I have an advantage—I'm in my early fifties and bald, so they can identify with me. When I talk one-on-one or address a group, they feel more comfortable and have less resistance to being tutored into the computer age."

As Florzak shows, if you keep up with the times, the waves of change can be as comfortable as gentle surf.

OVERCOMING INERTIA

Many Soft-Skilled Entrepreneurs are refugees from dying academic programs or other dead-end career tracks. For such people, escaping takes a lot of courage because they usually suffer two common fears: 1) that life outside the walls of the school or corporation will be lonely or lack intellectual stimulation; 2) that they can't survive on their own in the dog-eat-dog business world. Let's dispel these myths.

The SE defines the problem of loneliness as a chance to get to know oneself better, to test one's individual mettle. Academics quickly learn that their new role as SE provides no shortage of intellectual stimulation. In fact, business problems can inspire minds even more than scholarly problems because the former let you see results immediately. Anthropologist Richard Canter, for example, saw the academic pie continually shrinking and got "disgusted with the crumbs." So he formed a construction company that specializes in renovating urban apartments. Canter eventually came to see his work as a practical extension of his scholarly interests: "At first I was afraid that business wouldn't be as stimulating as academics. Then I discovered that being problem-oriented in business is just as important as it is in anthropology. There's more than enough of a challenge to keep you on your toes. Look at the concept of hierarchy. In our company of thirteen there's a definite hierarchy of skills, and you have to be able to give people their due without alienating anyone down the line. Being able to see it as an anthropological situation makes it easier to be sensitive to the people involved." Would he ever go back to the academic world? "Never!" Canter insists. "But I could if I wanted to—they don't take your Ph.D. away when you leave."

The same holds true for people languishing in the protective shadow of a corporation. As editor turned free-lance writer Jack Rochester points out, "Hell, I still enjoy the network of professional and personal relationships I developed working for publishing companies. And if I ever want to go back, I'd be a much more attractive employee now."

Concerning the second fear, that of survival in the ruthless business world, anyone who has struggled with academic politics and tenure battles will agree that academics make business people look tame by comparison. One SE, who holds a Ph.D. in Hindu philosophy and now runs a marketing research service, notes that "academic politics is probably the most vicious form of politics, because the stakes are so small. The academic world can be just as rough and tough a jungle as any business situation. Certainly your coworkers are much more critical in academia. You won't last too long if you have too thin a skin. We [Ph.D.s] have lots of experience and good backgrounds. We have already been tempered."

Jean Thomson, who holds a master's degree in English and now runs a technical communications firm, has this to say about the business environment: "When I grew up in the sixties I thought that academia was more honorable than business. But when I saw what was going on in academia, I realized that academics are as petty and backbiting as anyone else. There's actually something more honest about business. When you make a business deal with someone you know that you're both pretty much out for the same thing. There aren't as many delusions or pretenses."

Likewise, if you currently work for a corporation, you've seen your share of corporate politics and will find the outside world no more difficult to handle. Neil Duane, former head of technical writing for the Hewlett Packard Company, and now a partner in Boston Documentation Design, says that by the time he left Hewlett Packard he'd experienced about every kind of head-on clash he could imagine. "I was well prepared to deal with the world as the head of my firm," Duane says. "I just had to learn a few new tactics."

"See how the catfish skims along the river bottom," Master Hui said to Shen Ti as the two continued strolling down the banks of the river. "Because it rarely leaves the murky lower waters, it leads a life of contentment and safety. Should we envy the catfish's existence?"

"Perhaps," Shen Ti replied, "but only if we are satisfied with living off the scraps of others."

Scholar turned business writer. Donald Itkin (Madison, WI) yearned to become a scholar. Having graduated from college in the late sixties, he felt that only the academic life could allow him to retain his high values and ideals. Like many of his peers, Itkin also believed that business transformed humanists into spiritual vipers. So he packed his bags and went off to the University of Wisconsin in pursuit of Truth and a Ph.D. in English.

Six years later, Itkin, miserable, bored, and poor, was still working on his dissertation. When he married he found that the money he made as a teaching assistant couldn't support his small family, so he applied for several teaching positions, only to receive one insulting offer: a one-year teaching contract in New England for $10,000. Itkin reassessed his situation: "I finally decided," he recalls, "that if I wasn't going to live the idyllic life of a humanities professor on a shade-tree-lined street in a college town, I was going to make a decent living. This was a radical departure from everything I'd believed before, but it seemed right at the time."

Itkin set his sights on a career in business or industry and wrote four résumés he couldn't even afford to have printed. To make some extra money, he posted a number of advertisements around the university, offering to edit students' and professors' theses and articles. These efforts put enough cash in his pocket to finance the printing of two hundred résumés. The results? A mailboxful of rejections. But that didn't bother him, because his editorial service had begun to boom. He raised his rates and hired additional help. Soon he began receiving phone calls from business people in the surrounding community asking him to write for them.

Itkin discovered that while he couldn't charge academics more than $10 an hour, he could easily get $25 from business people. He also found that, without even realizing it, he'd become a business person himself. His editing service, "Wordcrafts," eventually evolved into an advertising agency that produces everything from graphics and ad copy to video and photography. "Suddenly we started getting calls to do advertising," boasts Itkin, "and that was where everything clicked. I realized we'd never get anywhere editing student dissertations and faculty books and that we should concentrate on promotional work. If anybody'd told me seven years ago that I'd be in advertising, I think I would have gotten sick."

Itkin, however, has no regrets about his six years in academia, because, as he says, "I learned how to learn. As a result I can absorb any kind of information very quickly. When you study literature, you're not just studying literature, you're studying everything: history, philosophy, science. I think everyone in advertising should get a master's in the humanities. You really need all that information."

More than simply transferring his skills from one field to another, Itkin has found that the diversity of his work actually challenges his intellectual limits. He's exploited his academic experience to attain the best of both worlds: he remains faithful to his love of the humanities, and he makes that "decent living" at the same time.

SE'S KNOW NO GENDER

Like perennial students and corporate serfs, many women have lived in the shadow of the home, but more and more are converting "domestic management" skills into fast-rising enterprises. "I know women who run their households far better than any executive could hope to run his business," says human-relations expert Dwight Platt, "but when they think of working, they think in terms of working for someone else. Instead of opening a secretarial service, they go to work as a secretary, where they're paid about one third what they're worth."

Like professional students, women often doubt their abilities to venture beyond traditional boundaries to become entrepreneurs. In large part, the hesitation stems from the outdated belief that men are the innovators and that entrepreneurship is a male domain. Some myths crumble quickly in the Techno Age; women entrepreneurs rank equal to or better than their male counterparts in terms of creativity, financial success, and the ability to manage. And as you'll soon see, at least half of the SE's profiled in this book are women. Still, women do encounter some special problems.

The most common objections women raise? "How can I possibly start a business? I've spent ten [or twenty or thirty] years as a mother [or teacher, or secretary]. I haven't the slightest idea where to begin. I have absolutely no business experience." As all SE's discover, you can learn whatever you need to know by doing and asking. A business degree doesn't guarantee success, and it may even be a barrier to success. Gayle Moeller, who helped conceive and develop a brilliant idea for a chain of airport spas, puts it this way: "Being less experienced and less skilled has actually been to our benefit, because my partner and I thought that anything was possible. We overcame our inexperience with research. It was a process of seeking out those people with the insight and experience to answer the questions we *had* to know. We learned that persistence is one of our best assets. Anybody can make it if they dig deep enough and stick to it."

One woman who persisted is Kathleen Diamond. After receiving a master's degree in French literature, Diamond assumed she'd find a job teaching French, preferably in a nonacademic setting. "I went to Berlitz," she says, "and they wanted to pay me $4.80 an hour. I was enraged and decided there had to be some solution. And when I didn't see any, I set about making one myself." The result was Language Learning Enterprises, which offers private instruction in a variety of languages. To start the school Diamond put a help-wanted ad in *The Washington Post* and spent six days interviewing other language instructors in local coffee shops. Then, with $1,000 from her savings account, she bought the equipment she needed. Within two years Language Learning Enterprises grew by leaps and bounds, out of Diamond's living room into the greater Washington metropolitan area. The school now has contracts with the federal government to teach diplomats more than fifty foreign languages. As Diamond says, "The most difficult translation is turning your desires into something that really touches people. Everybody *wants* something. The difference is in really making it happen."

Some women see money as the major obstacle to making things happen. "I was never good at math," many say, "and business people have to be able to perform all sorts of financial wheelings and dealings." Wrong. If you can balance a checkbook, budget your family's money to pay for groceries out of one pocket and clothes out of another, then you can maintain a ledger. Besides, an accountant will set up your books and show you how to make the necessary entries. Most women are far better financial managers than they realize.

An important aspect of the funding issue has to do with finding seed money. Only in recent years have equal credit opportunities for women become a reality, so many women still can't imagine raising the capital to start a venture. Most SE's, however, get their seed money from nontraditional sources, such as friends and family, loyal customers, and trusting suppliers. *Any* SE can raise capital using the techniques illustrated in Chapter 5. As Brenda Ellis, who started a cooperative office suite, says, "I found out there's loads of money out there. You just have to figure out where to get it."

Finally, women have to learn to take risks. As relative newcomers to the business world, women tend to take fewer risks than men. So while most women's SE projects may be less likely to crash completely, they also tend to fall short of their highest potential. Risk and reward go hand in hand. Brenda Ellis says you have to throw your devotion to financial security overboard: "I know I can never fail as a person. If my business fails, my mother will still love me, my boyfriend will still love me, and my dog will still love me. I might have to waitress for a while. But I certainly won't starve."

"The river offers the lessons of both weakness and strength," Master Hui commented to Shen Ti. *"Can you explain how something can embody such apparent opposites?"*

"That is the essence of yin and yang," Shen Ti replied. *"Although the water may display the softness, gentleness, and pliancy of yin, it also has the power and strength of yang. It slips through your fingers but it also moves mountains."*

Master Hui smiled approvingly. *"Then you understand how strength lies within weakness, and weakness within strength."*

Perfect to the letter. "From the time I was four," says Regina Collinsgru, "I knew I wanted to have my own business. It's just in my personality—I can't stand someone else telling me what to do." It took almost seven years as a secretary and a volunteer, however, before Collinsgru took the plunge.

"My last job was at the Harvard Business School," she says, "and I hated it. I sat behind a desk all day and watched people coming in and out who were not much older or smarter than me, and they were doing all these exciting things." Still, Collinsgru stuck it out at Harvard for three years before she decided it was time to break loose.

After three months of thinking about ways to apply her skills in a timely way, Collinsgru decided that a word-processing service would combine her secretarial experience with advanced but newly affordable technologies. So she wrote a business plan, borrowed $8,000 in seed money from friends and relatives, quit her secretarial job, and moved into a storefront down the street from the business school. In the fall of 1979 she opened the doors of Letter Perfect Office Services, which provides word-processing service to Harvard and the surrounding business community. In its first year Letter Perfect Office Services grossed $35,000, and Collinsgru projects revenues of $200,000 for 1984.

In many ways Collinsgru sees herself as a typical female entrepreneur, confronting many of the business problems women face when dealing with money. "Men usually get into business for profitability," she says, "while women tend to focus on things like control, flexibility, and expression. Women are generally afraid to put a price tag on themselves—they're afraid of becoming narrow-minded business people. I know that I was scared to death of sacrificing my values for the business."

Over the years, Collinsgru has altered her position. Instead of stereotyping entrepreneurs as "cutthroat," she has come to appreciate their shrewd business thinking, and prides herself on being as tough as they come. Did her years as a secretary go to waste? Not for an instant. She feels that her experience as a service person enabled her to deal with details and management problems in a confident but attentive way, something she thinks men have a harder time doing. Collinsgru illustrates that a woman can put her talents to work for herself instead of giving them over to a boss who would never pay her adequately.

ON BECOMING A SOFT-SKILLED ENTREPRENEUR: RIGHT WORKING

As you'll see in the following chapters, anyone can learn to devise, develop, and market successful SE projects, but it takes more than simply putting the techniques into practice. While the techniques are important, they work best if you first adopt certain attitudes that promote a balanced relationship between yourself and the world around you. Such balance separates the Soft-Skilled Entrepreneurs from business people who see personal gain as the ultimate goal, life itself as a zero-sum proposition: "For me to win, someone else must lose." In contrast, SE's see their own gain as everyone's gain, and they look for situations that offer such possibilities: "For me to win, how can I best harmonize with the people, things, and resources around me?"

This attitude is nicely stated by SE Alex Randall, founder of the Boston Computer Exchange. "My idea of entrepreneurship is the 'plus sum game,' which means that everyone comes out with what they want. This isn't dreaming; all you have to do is start off looking for ways for everyone to come out ahead, rather than looking for personal bottom-line profit projections. It's just a matter of your orientation." Bob Kuzara, a wizard at financing businesses with no money down, agrees. "The name of the game is win-win. It really doesn't have to be any different."

Such thinking parallels the Zen notion of "right working," which essentially means acting in a way that resonates with your immediate environment (including your internal beliefs, goals, and values). How does one achieve this "personal resonance"? Let's say you really don't like or understand computers but discover you could make a lot of money setting up a software store in a new shopping center. You borrow some money and open the store. The business shows some signs of life, you hire a manager, then you sell the store to someone with more interest in computers. A successful project, right? Wrong. It may have succeeded in a superficial way, but it failed in a more important way: you wasted valuable time and energy that could have been invested in a project engaging your heart, soul, and creative energies, thereby providing a deep and abiding satisfaction. Moreover, you've contributed little to the community in which you opened the store because you did not add imagination and value. All you cared about was a fast buck. If you really believed in the utility and value of software, you would have thrown yourself into the project and invented something much more meaningful (and, ultimately, more profitable) than a quick kill. In short, you could have created an extension of yourself, making a contribution to your personal growth and the surrounding community.

Master Hui and Shen Ti watched a swift cat toying with a mouse on the riverbank.

"The cat teaches us an important lesson," Shen Ti remarked.

"Yes," Master Hui agreed. "Work hard and play hard."

Shen Ti laughed. "True, but I had a different lesson in mind: Let work be play, and play be work!"

The following Rules for Right Working demonstrate various ways that SE's engage in their work. Note how success in each case goes well beyond monetary gain and embodies a deep sense of personal accomplishment and satisfaction.

Rule 1: Undertake Projects That Make You Proud.
A project can succeed only if you put yourself behind it 100 percent. And you can do that only if you truly believe in what you're doing.

Turning good words into a good living. Literary agent H. Michael Snell (Wayland, MA) ultimately went into the business of developing and selling book ideas because he wanted to help good authors bring good books to the public. After finishing his bachelor's degree in English literature, Snell thought about going on for a master's degree but was coaxed by an insightful professor to try his hand at publishing, which might allow him to more profitably benefit from his love of English. Snell followed the suggestion, but after working at a major publishing house as a textbook editor for thirteen years, he saw that becoming a literary agent would provide the opportunity to get more involved with authors and expose him to a wider range of topics. Today he brings in more than $750,000 in advances and royalties for his authors each year, and his commission on those sums more than affords him the kind of life-style he desires.

Snell attributes his success to two main factors: "Most of the books I represent are designed to help readers solve their business or personal problems or improve the quality of their lives. The money is nice, but it's only one measure of my contribution to the reading public. The real payoff comes from knowing that I've turned a rough idea into a lasting resource that benefits other people."

Rule 2: Never Allow Work to Be Work.
SE's never distinguish between vocation and avocation, but rather forge their work and their passions into a durable alloy.

From Italy with love. Retired artist and teacher Frieda Yamins (Freeport, NY) first went to Europe when she was thirty-six years old to actually *see* the works she'd read about in art-history textbooks. After falling madly in love with the city of Florence, she resolved to make an annual trip to Italy to paint, make friends, and learn Italian. Were these unconventional plans for a housewife/teacher in the New York public-school system in 1962? Perhaps, but her friends admired her for so dedicatedly "advancing her studies."

In 1979 an unexpected opportunity catapulted her into SEdom. Appreciating her European experience, her school's administration invited her to help plan an Italian trip for the school chorus. Given Frieda's knowledge of the country, the chorus enjoyed a memorable excursion, and next year's chorus found it even more exciting.

From these beginnings sprang Italia Adagio (Italy Slowly), a service that offers the finest possible tours of Italy, every detail painstakingly planned, every restaurant personally sampled, every rest stop scrutinized. Carefully selected classical music piped through the tour bus sets the perfect mood as the bus rolls into a new city on the most beautiful approach. In five years the idea has rocketed Yamins's $500 initial publicity budget (a loan from an uncle) to $1 million a year in sales.

Italia Adagio has enabled Yamins not only to retire from the school system and live substantially better than a schoolteacher's pension would have afforded but also to live and work with her first love in life. Says Yamins, "The arts have always been the most important thing to me, and I think of my tours as works of art. Every little refinement is an attempt to make them more beautiful. That's why I love tending to the little details myself— the final product is an artistic expression of myself."

Rule 3: Let Passion Stir You, Reason Guide You.

When SE's undertake projects, they feel a surge of excitement and exhilaration akin to falling in love. Tempered by reason, such passion brings unparalleled success.

The saga of an unemployable philosopher. "I looked in the classified-ad sections and couldn't find one single job opening for a philosopher," recalls Martin Dean (Kentfield, CA), "so I went to law school." By the time Dean finished, he had spent nine years at the University of Wisconsin, balancing his lengthy schooling with a diversity of legal specialties from trial to show-business law.

Like most lawyers in the eighties, Dean saw the wisdom of

using a word processor to draft his documents, but he quickly grew disenchanted with the technology because all the software he tried was either too simple to be useful or too complex to learn easily. Fueled by a true entrepreneurial spirit, Martin decided to fill the gap by assigning two programmers the task of creating an easy-to-learn yet powerful legal-word-processing package. Eight months later Martin, with a completed software program in hand, formed Select Information Systems, which later merged with Summa Technologies and acquired a staff of fifty. Martin serves as Summa's Chairman of the Board.

As Martin retells it, his inspiration for creating a better legal-word-processing program was an almost civic duty: "Outrage! I was performing on television as a consumer-rights advocate and a computer-software consumer. I saw that word-processing programs were being manufactured by people who didn't have to use them—they made their programs complicated, difficult, and unfriendly. I got angry every time I sat down at the keyboard. The only way I could relieve that anger was to get involved with designing a program that people could look at and say, 'Yes, I can use this!'" Judging from the $1.5 million in first-year sales of the Select word-processing package and the fact that his company was able to introduce a hot-selling advanced version called "Free Style," Martin has achieved his goal and made a lasting mark in the Techno Age.

Rule 4: Give Back What You Take.

One way or another, SE's repay those who make their projects possible, be they benefactors, employees, friends, teachers, or the community.

From busboy to boss. "If life is a stage, I want to be the director," says Norman S. Shum (Dallas, TX), who founded China Belle, the first Chinese fast-food chain in the Dallas area. Shum had previously worked as a busboy at a local Sheraton hotel, where he was depressed over the prospect of working for thirty years and ending up with a gold watch (as the Sheraton's manager did). So he conceived the idea of selling Chinese fast food at a large shopping mall. After garnering permission from the mall's leasing agent to operate his project out of a defunct fried-chicken store, he pulled together enough money from a bank loan and his friends to start his business. And to make up for his lack of retailing experience, he sought the advice of others in the mall—clerks at various stores—to find out what consumers enjoyed. "Impulse buying" seemed to be the universal answer, so Shum created a display kitchen concept for passersby that proved so irresistible to their impulses that China Belle has expanded into four other malls, with Shum planning to set up fifteen more in the next year and seventy-five stores in the next five years, along with a new national franchising program for entrepreneurs.

The owner demonstrates his gratitude to his real benefactors, the public, in a unique way. Although China Belle demands round-the-clock attention, Shum sets time aside to run a college advisory and career-development service for his employees. Says Shum: "The biggest reward for me is being in a position where I can go out and help other people, and give back what I received from the society. Then there's being able to say, 'The American dream is alive and well,' and to prove it by creating something out of nothing. That's the best satisfaction I can possibly have."

Rule 5: See Personal Growth as the Highest Form of Achievement.

SE's do desire money and the creature comforts it can buy. But they seek self-fulfillment above all material success.

Living-room gold. Dwight Platt (Baltimore, MD) finished the Great Books program at St. John's College in 1970. He missed the application deadlines for law school ("that great stomping ground for undirected generalists") and found himself enrolled in a seminary ("a less popular but more erudite stomping ground for undirected generalists").

By December of his first year, Platt became dissatisfied with his theological studies and, after gathering his life savings, decided to see how a generalist could fare in the specific world of business. He based his first idea on a newly emerging trend in pop psychology called "self-awareness," which had been introduced by the best-selling book *I'm OK, You're OK*. With absolutely no previous experience, Platt put together human-relations programs for businesses, modeled after his college seminars and

designed to close communication gaps and solve interpersonal di-
lemmas, thereby promoting corporate growth.

Platt found that for every two hundred sales calls he made,
he would end up with one contract. Still, that got the enterprise
rolling, and his first year he earned $25,000. Within five years his
annual income rose to $130,000. By that time he had a wife, two
children, a car, and a mortgage. He was also growing bored: "As
long as I was reading and researching, and developing new programs, it was a thrill. But the problems I saw in 1970 and the
problems I saw in 1975 were very much the same—I was doing
the same thing over and over. To me that was a no-growth situation."

Platt unexpectedly found the answer to his boredom in real
estate. Although he began investing in property as a tax shelter,
he started making money from it and was soon surprised to find
himself intrigued with the mechanics of real estate. Before long
he began winding down his consulting business to afford more
time for developing residential property. All this regained for
Platt the thrill he'd lost. "Real estate is full of factors you can't
control," he says, "so it keeps your adrenaline flowing. There's no
danger of getting bored if at any second your savings could just
roll right out the door."

Drawn by the riskiness of his new enterprise, Platt began
working double time and made a handsome sum building town
houses in Baltimore at the peak of the real-estate boom. But
while his business grew stronger, his marriage began crumbling,
and in 1982 Platt suddenly found himself with the full responsibility for a household and two small boys. Shocked and confused,
Platt ground his business to a shuddering halt while he took stock
of his priorities. It didn't take him long to realize that above all
else he needed to be at home with his children. So he sold his
shares in the real-estate company to his partner and looked for a
way to manage commercial real estate from his home.

Platt's divorce forced him to rediscover an important value:
his family. He found that by working at home he got to know his
sons, while simultaneously learning a new and stimulating aspect of his business. Looking back, Platt advises entrepreneurs to
take stock of their personal goals and ideals *before* diving into an
all-consuming project: "If you're going to work eighty hours a
week, you'd better take time to make sure that what you're work-

ing for is what you want to get. In 1975 I could easily measure how much money and material success I'd built up. One of the things I had more difficulty seeing was whether my businesses gave me what I needed in terms of my personal growth and development. And it turned out that I almost missed it."

SUCCESS DEPENDS ON PERSISTENCE, NOT GENIUS

Parenting an SE project takes time and effort. Many turn out to be difficult births, even for veteran SE's who know the fine points of cesarean delivery. And regardless of the midwifery skills involved, some projects will be stillborn, while others will survive but grow into problem children that sap your strength and energy.

A bleak picture? Not for the SE; tough odds mean greater challenges, and greater challenges reap higher rewards. In any case, the SE never throws in the towel. He or she may crawl back to the drawing board drained or slightly confused but always having learned from a mistake, always with a stronger resolve to win next time.

Veteran SE's will tell you that success depends on keeping up the good fight or attacking a different battlefield. Rohn Engh (Osceola, WI), who publishes the *Photoletter*, nicely sums up this point: "To succeed you don't have to be a person of special talents, know the right people, or be in the right geographical region. The people who succeed are the ones who follow through—the ones who stick it out and hang in by their fingernails, the ones who pick themselves up even after they've been knocked down for the fiftieth time. No, the problem is never failing, it's quitting."

Master Hui and his disciple began the long walk back home.
"I have learned much today," Shen Ti said to his teacher.
"But one thing bothers me."
Master Hui paused. "And what is that?"
"Where does the river end?"

"You surprise me, Shen Ti," the Master said. "Great rivers never end, they just keep flowing forever."

A preview of success. When Sharon Arkin (Silver Spring, MD) took a master's degree in counseling, she never imagined herself becoming an entrepreneur. But after two years of running a counseling and referral service for a large federal agency, her dissatisfaction with the referral system catapulted her into a creative and promising SE project.

Arkin had found she often referred clients to therapists whose treatment philosophy or clinical practices were not very well known to her. "I'd meet them at the social hour of professional meetings and they'd hand me a business card, hoping for referrals. I had no idea what these therapists did in the privacy of the therapy hour."

One day, while reading a newspaper article about Georgetown Connection, a video dating service in Washington, DC, a light bulb tripped on in Arkin's head: now that video dating is a popular and accepted way to match people, why not use a similar concept to match clients and therapists? She introduced this Techno Age idea at a meeting of associated therapists, asking for volunteers. When twenty people signed up, Therapist Preview was born.

Therapist Preview's approach is based on solid research evidence that positive therapy outcomes depend on a good "match" between client and therapist. Such a match requires compatibility of personality, values, and style of communication. Therapist Preview enables a prospective client to watch videotaped interviews with therapists and study detailed résumés they have completed.

Prior to the appointment, a client completes a detailed questionnaire about the symptoms and history of the problem, personal assets and liabilities, and therapy goals. During a two-hour session, Arkin reviews the questionnaire with the client, presents five or six selections from her videotape library, helps the client evaluate the information presented and come to a decision. At the end of the session, which costs $120, a client usually feels comfortable about choosing a therapist.

Despite the ingenuity of the idea, Arkin found herself battling some unforeseen demons. First, since insurance companies will not cover the cost of her service, her clients must pay the full amount themselves, and many can't afford the fee. Arkin hopes to affiliate with a psychiatrist and thereby lick the insurance problem. A more serious challenge, however, arose from the discovery that although medical advertising is now deemed ethical and legal, most psychiatrists and therapists look down on it. And to add insult to injury, the major psychiatric journals would not even *accept* her advertisements.

Undaunted by the resistance of the medical community, Arkin decided to try another tack, placing an enticing advertisement in a Washington newspaper under the headline "Is Your Therapist Outstanding? Recommend Him/Her to Therapist Preview." The response was excellent, and Arkin accumulated a list of some two hundred recommended therapists. She then went door to door, asking these therapists if they would agree to be interviewed on tape. To her delight, more than fifty agreed.

Two years have passed since Arkin began trying to persuade psychiatrists and therapists of the service's usefulness, and now, with a varied roster of seventy-five outstanding therapists, she can provide many suitable choices to an array of clients. Though still operating on slender margins, she's convinced that her idea will eventually triumph. And with that kind of commitment she's already a winner.

EXERCISE 1.1: RATE YOUR SE POTENTIAL

Complete each of the following twelve statements by selecting the letter that most accurately describes you and your views. Then score each statement, total your results, and evaluate your potential for becoming an SE at the end of the exercise.

1. Success depends on:

   a. where/when you were born

   b. previous business experience

   c. your parents' life-style

   d. your educational experience

    e. all of the above

    f. none of the above

2. Your perceptions of the world:

    a. are forever changing

    b. are formed during the first few years of your life

    c. are those of your parents and teachers

    d. remain relatively constant once formed

    e. vary with your moods

3. When you read the newspaper you:

    a. read from cover to cover

    b. skip the local news

    c. read only the comics

    d. read just the business section

    e. find it boring

    f. like to read about clever inventions

4. When you read or hear about unusual inventions you usually think:

    a. How ridiculous!

    b. People will buy anything!

    c. I could have come up with that!

    d. What will they think of next!

    e. It's only a fad!

5. You often find yourself frustrated by the lack of a certain product or service and say to yourself, "Why doesn't somebody come up with a ____?"

a. often

b. sometimes

c. rarely

d. never

6. If something interests you, but is not in your area of expertise, you:

   a. ask somebody to explain it to you

   b. read a book or article about it anyway

   c. forget about it

   d. think about it a lot

7. Ferdinand Demara, "the great impostor," is:

   a. dead

   b. an inexpensive Italian wine that tastes expensive

   c. a dangerous psychopath

   d. a hero

   e. an all-around good guy

8. The idea that "everyone has a price tag," a dollar amount for which he or she would do something that compromises his or her most cherished values, is:

   a. true

   b. sad but true

   c. pretty likely

   d. probably false

   e. nonsense

9. You value the freedom to shape the environment in which you work, but this is a luxury which can be offset by:

a. monetary compensation

b. power

c. prestige/fame

d. convenience

e. any/all of the above

f. no compromise

10. When you start a job or project:

a. you finish it as quickly as possible

b. it doesn't matter what it is, it's worth maximum effort

c. you find it difficult to finish

d. you are in the middle of many other projects

11. Work is:

a. a necessary evil

b. an integral part of life

c. a means of learning and personal growth

12. When you believe in something you:

a. tell everybody around you

b. make your opinion clear to those who ask

c. stick with it through thick and thin

Scoring:

Check your answers against the key below. Note that a low score won't prevent you from achieving great success as an SE as long as you are willing to learn, and work hard.

Statement	Answers	Value	Your Score
1	a–d	0	
	e	1	
	f	5	
2	a	5	
	b,c	2	
	d,e	0	
3	a,f	5	
	d	3	
	b,c,e	0	
4	a,d,e	0	
	b	1	
	c	5	
5	a	5	
	b	3	
	c	1	
	d	0	
6	a	2	
	b	5	
	c,d	0	
7	a,b,c	0	
	e	1	
	d	5	
8	a–d	0	
	e	5	
9	a–e	0	
	f	5	
10	a,c	0	
	b	5	
	d	2	

11	a	0
	b,c	5
12	a	0
	b,c	5

Total score:

above 55:	Grade-A SE stock.
45 to 54:	You'll definitely make a good SE after you realize a little more of your potential.
35 to 44:	You'll probably make it as an SE. But pay particular attention to Chapter 2.
25 to 34:	Move cautiously before starting an SE project. Build up your confidence and supply yourself with a good safety net.
15 to 24:	Work hard at rearranging your priorities and goals before considering an SE life-style.
Below 15:	The SE life-style may not be for you.

EXERCISE 1.2: LOOKING FOR SE'S IN THE WORLD ABOUT YOU

For the next few days scan your favorite newspapers and magazines with new eyes: look for Soft-Skilled Entrepreneur projects. You should also study *The Wall Street Journal, Venture, Inc.*, and other general business publications that you might not have read in the past. Every time you spot an SE, note how he or she fits the general profiles described in this chapter. Can you imagine yourself doing something similar? How do you think it would feel? Carry that feeling with you as you work through the next chapter on developing a good SE mind-set.

2
FREE-SPIRIT LIBERATION: LEARNING TO TURN RISK INTO ADVENTURE

Summer gently rolled into the valley, bringing long sun-drenched days and mild nights. Moved by the lush green hues decorating mountain and valley, Master Hui called together his students for a discourse on the vastness of nature.

"Behold the greatness of Mount Tang," the Master said, pointing to a majestic peak in the distance. "See how it disappears into the clouds toward the very end of the sky. Imagine yourselves gazing down at the earth from the top of the mountain where falcons nest. As you fathomed the essence of the distance below, you would truly sense the grand scale of our world."

"To me," said disciple Shen Ti, "it would all seem quite small."

"And how can that be?" Master Hui asked.

"Because," Shen explained, "if I were to look down from the top of old Tang I would surely become dizzy and fall flat on my back. Then, as I peered into the depth of the heavens, the mountain and all below would seem little more than an anthill!"

"True enough!" the Master agreed with a laugh. "In your own way you have demonstrated how much depends on one's point of view."

YOU ARE WHAT YOU THINK

Everything in life depends on your point of view. Take a cow. To a motorist speeding down a Kansas interstate, a cow crossing the highway spells danger; but to a Masai warrior, whose universe revolves around cattle, a cow offers so many rich possibilities that he has many different words for it. Or take ice. To an arctic explorer, it could pose a deadly threat, while to a parched prospector crawling through Death Valley it could mean survival.

Modern physicists have pushed the relativity notion one step further, claiming that we *actually create reality with our minds*. "Voodoo magic," you say? Sure. Voodoo works because the victim *believes* it will work, and the victim's mind, through a process not yet understood, whips up a neurochemical hurricane that stops the heart and lungs dead. Voodoo victims literally scare themselves to death.

By the same token, of course, any nurse will tell you that a patient's survival depends as much on the will to live as on the surgeon's knife. In fact, research has shown that a startling number of surgical patients who think they will not survive an operation actually don't, while others clinging steadfastly to their wills to live, do. In the same vein, a keen sense of humor, as Norman Cousins shows in his book *Anatomy of an Illness*, can work more wonders than medical-miracle cures. Some medical journals are also now touting the use of visualization and guided mental imagery (such as scenes of strong white cells gobbling up cancer cells) as effective weapons against seemingly hopeless diseases.

Soft-Skilled Entrepreneurs not only know all about such powers of positive thinking; they've made them essential tools in their arsenals. Knowing that the right mind-set can counter years of bad habits and self-defeating outlooks, SE's force themselves to consider many perspectives of a given problem or situation. To the SE a glass of water is always half-full, never half-empty.

For instance, when SE Jack Rochester found himself with a lucrative Techno Age opportunity to rewrite user's manuals for Coleco's Adam computer, he might have said, "I can't handle it—I don't know BASIC programming." Instead, he relied on his communication and learning skills and hooked up with a programming genius who taught him the technical details he needed to do the job. Rochester not only completed the assignment but also wrote a better book because of the circumstances. "I think I was much more sensitive to the naive user because I had just learned the technical stuff myself," he says. As Rochester demonstrates, adversity can be transformed into prosperity with just a flip of the mind switch.

Fortunately, anyone can learn to adopt the positive perspective that enables so many SE's to succeed. With that outlook to guide you, you can break out of conventional molds and create realities in which your financial and life-style dreams come true. The next section provides the tools you'll need to make the transition from voodoo victim to powerful master of your own fate. And with your new mind-set, you'll have the most important equipment you need to carve out a unique Techno Age niche.

A SIX-PART PROCESS FOR ACHIEVING A POSITIVE MIND-SET

You begin the process at the core of your being, meditating on old habits until you can see them from a fresh point of view. Once you've eradicated self-defeating thoughts, you'll replace them with affirmations and images that support a self-fulfilling future. You'll then learn how to forge a new and fuller identity from your unique strengths rather than from external sources such as work or school. The fourth phase emphasizes risks as healthy adventures rather than life-threatening dangers, and the fifth teaches the value of "beneficial compromises." The final phase encourages you to listen to and trust the ultimate inner guide: your free spirit.

Phase 1: Zap Negative Thoughts: The Domino Effect
If you accept the fact that you create your own reality with your mind, you can see the importance of identifying and eliminating any thoughts and feelings that prevent you from using your existing skills and abilities to their fullest. Given the number of mental barriers most people set up for themselves over the years, this may at first appear a formidable task. But once you successfully knock over a few "half-empty" thoughts, you'll find all the others tumbling down in their path.

To stimulate this domino effect, analyze your everyday language, searching for words that reflect a hidden negative mindset. Search out and destroy the negative words and phrases you commonly use to define the glass as half-empty rather than half-full, such as the "Seven Deadly Mind Traps":

1. Only people with _____ can do _____.
2. I haven't been trained to _____.
3. I'm too old to _____.
4. I'm too young to _____.
5. I couldn't imagine myself _____.
6. I have no aptitude for _____.
7. I'm not cut out to _____.

Such phrases provide convenient, but poor, excuses for maintaining the status quo in your life, because they all boil down to the self-defeating illusion that "I can't because I can't." In short, they trap you into trapping yourself.

How often does one or more of the Seven Deadly Mind Traps run through your head? Probably more often than you think. Carry a notebook around for a few days and jot down every occasion when you speak or think in self-negating terms. You'll be surprised at the consistent pattern that emerges. And that's good; just seeing the pattern will help you begin dismantling it.

Most of us fall into mind traps because, in large part, we've been taught to specialize at a ridiculously early age. Even in elementary school we're pigeonholed according to our apparent aptitudes and talents, encouraged to do what others think we do best. Throughout high school we focus on our strengths and shun our alleged weaknesses. And by college, which is supposed to be a time of great exploration, most of us are deeply entrenched in a career path that we began many years before. How many potential Glenn Goulds or Eudora Weltys have wound up in medical or law school? Brian Smith, former IBM engineer turned consultant and writer, sums it up this way: "Many people have funny notions about themselves that are really erroneous, such as the idea that they're limited. That happens because one of the terrible things our society teaches people when they're young is what they can't do. Ninety percent of what you learn is what you're supposedly not able to do—you just have to throw that kind of thinking away."

Other SE's point to the fear of failure as a major source of mind-trapping thoughts. Irene Smalls, who started her own marketing and PR firm, offers an ingenious method for keeping such fears from paralyzing you: "I've taught a lot of self-assessment courses," she comments, "and shown many people how to write a 'demon paper.' A demon paper acknowledges that we all have demons—basic fears—that drive us. Everybody has them. The idea is not to try to get rid of the demons, but to hold them by the hand and say, 'Okay, I know you're here and I know what you're about. But we have to do this anyway, so let's just hold hands and go.'"

On the other side of the coin, a hidden fear of success often propels people to create mind traps that say they don't somehow *deserve* to succeed. Chocolate-chip-cookie impresario Wally Amos puts it this way: "So many of us are conditioned to think that you have to become a tragic character before you can achieve anything. That's just not true—everyone is worthy of success. If you believe in yourself and you're committed to what you're doing, you're entitled to succeed. It's up to you!"

And philosopher turned entrepreneur Charles Levin, who now develops business software, cites yet another source of mind traps, which he calls the "personal-entropy" syndrome: "Entropy is the idea that nature moves in the direction of lowest states of energy; things always change in a way that allows them to expend less and less energy. The same can happen to people throughout the course of their lives. There's a natural tendency to take the path of least resistance, to spend as little energy as possible by saying 'No,' 'I can't,' or 'Let's not.' Personal entropy poses the greatest threat to success, and the only way to overcome it is to force yourself to ever-higher energy states through projects of your own making."

In addition to unlearning past conditioning and working against entropy, you must pinpoint the mind traps that others bestow upon you through their own negative thinking. Unsupportive, unimaginative, or downright jealous friends and family deter many potential SE's from their self-liberation. "You could never pull that off," and "What do you know about psychother-

malnucleonics?" often come from people who think they're looking out for your best interests. Almost every successful SE can
recall at least one person who said "Don't do it" or "You'll lose
your shirt." Martin Dean, for instance, remembers how numerous people told him not to start his software company: "There's
an anti-new-business mentality that you have to overcome,"
Dean says, "especially from people who are in business themselves. They look back and think about all the hard work they
had to do, and forget all the excitement they experienced. Probably they're just burnt out—they don't remember how excitement
and the high energy that goes with it are major factors in getting
off the ground."

Marc Bender, a media consultant, also warns about the danger of negative thoughts generated by those around you: "Most
people, even friends, are threatened on some level by the idea of
the entrepreneur, successful or not. They may not understand
why or how you're doing what you're doing. They may fear that
by taking the path less traveled, you're drifting out of their lives.
All they know for certain is that you're 'different.' I have many
friends who work for corporations and have the things I lack:
stability, a steady income, the synergy of their offices. Yet whenever I sit down with them, they babble on about my freedom and
independence, and I sense something wistful about it. I detect a
trace of jealousy or resentment there, too. So I take people's reactions to my new ideas very guardedly. . . . I never internalize
them or confuse them with my own feelings."

With all these sources of negative thinking, how can you
ever remain positive? One answer comes from Robert Schwartz,
who has masterminded a number of lucrative entrepreneurial
ventures: "The greatest obstacle to success is ultimately yourself.
Parts of you want to win, but parts want to lose. The loser parts
say, 'This is a drain, this is a crazy idea, this can't work.' You just
have to fight for the parts that want to win."

If the negative forces seem hopelessly overpowering, just remember that the war is made up of many battles. You can't ex-
pect to zap all your negative thoughts and undo the draining
effects of others overnight. Work on language, work on putting
other people's negative views into perspective, and then work on
putting your own fears to sleep. In time you will find yourself at

peace with all your demons, so much so that you won't even recognize their presence.

"Why do mice always scamper for cover?" Master Hui asked Shen Ti as the two sipped tea and watched the sun set behind Mount Tang.

"Fear?" offered Shen Ti.

"Yes, but their fear springs from a point of view that defines the world as huge and dangerous."

Shen Ti shook his head. "If I were a mouse I'd pretend to be a falcon perched high on the mountainside. Then the world would look like a table set for a feast."

The tale of a resourceful matchmaker. Vicki Mechner (Chappaqua, NY) ventured into the business world quite by accident. It all started when her children changed schools. "There were seven hundred kids in this school," she explains, "and all of them had parents who were skilled or talented at something. And the school just wasn't taking advantage of all the resources the parents had to offer." After interviewing a number of parents, Mechner set up a resource center in the school's library. Soon parents were giving guest lectures, working as teachers' aides, participating in the after-school program, and doing far more than the traditional chores of baking cookies and driving car pools.

Pleased with her success, Mechner worked on a similar project in her community, giving the townspeople access to each other's time and talents. Business people found secretaries, filmmakers found models, parents found baby-sitters.

Recognizing her talent for resource brokering, Mechner formed OmniQuest, Inc., an information-search service based in her own home. Her hope was to match buyers and sellers—to match consultant seekers with consultants, carousel buyers with carousel sellers. Without a lot of clients, however, it was difficult to match anything with anybody. So Mechner found herself doing a lot of time-consuming research on her own to satisfy the needs of her clients. Despite the problems, Mechner stuck with OmniQuest for about seven years, willing to stay relatively small and willing to do specialized research.

On the surface, staying small gave Mechner the opportunity to spend time with friends and family. But looking back on it, Mechner realizes that she pursued OmniQuest partly *because* she knew it would never grow big and would never exist independently of her. "My husband is an entrepreneur," she says, "and I could see how completely engrossing it is for him, to the exclusion of everything else. I was limiting myself to keep the business from taking over. I guess I just got over that."

Mechner's new enterprise is a refined version of OmniQuest, called PartnerQuest. Instead of matching buyers with sellers, she matches people with people. "*Everyone* needs a partner," she says, "whether it's a business partner or a social partner. Unlike OmniQuest, it doesn't take a half hour to explain the new service. The whole thing is coded and computerized, so there's no need for expensive specialized research. Instead, I put my research skills into developing the forty-eight-page questionnaire that each subscriber has to fill out. Sophisticated software takes care of the rest."

Mechner hopes to have 30,000 subscribers to PartnerQuest, and at $50 per subscription, it is evident that she is no longer limiting herself to stay small. She doesn't dare to project her next year's net income, but as she says, "Even the most pessimistic figures are embarrassingly huge."

Phase 2: Shape a Healthy Mind-Set: The Power of Positive Affirmation

Once you've cleared your mental screen of self-defeating attitudes and negative language, you can begin to paint it with constructive thoughts and positive expressions. Don't mistake this activity for simple-minded optimism or the rose-colored-glasses syndrome. Rather, see it as the painstaking and deliberate creation of desirable realities that can help you achieve what you want in life. Just as in zapping a negative mind-set, one begins with language that will mirror positive thoughts.

Think back to the Seven Deadly Mind Traps in Phase 1. Try recasting them into Mind Lifts—nurturing, positive statements that counter the effects of personal entropy and other self-negating phenomena:

Mind Trap 1. Only people with ____ can do ____.
Mind Lift 1. I can easily transfer my skills in ____ so that I can ____.
Mind Trap 2. I haven't been trained to ____.
Mind Lift 2. My expertise lies in ____, but I've got the energy and intelligence to learn ____.
Mind Trap 3. I'm too old to ____.
Mind Lift 3. My lifelong experience will help me to ____.
Mind Trap 4. I'm too young to ____.
Mind Lift 4. My eagerness and energy will enable me to ____.
Mind Trap 5. I couldn't imagine myself ____.
Mind Lift 5. Since I create my own reality, I can easily see myself ____.
Mind Trap 6. I have no aptitude for ____.
Mind Lift 6. With a little extra effort I'll master ____.
Mind Trap 7. I'm not cut out to ____.
Mind Lift 7. When the need arises, I'll be able to ____.

Even after using such positive language for only a few days, you'll see many stumbling blocks crumbling to dust. Then you can sweep up the rubble and adopt a new, positive mind-set.

Positive mental phrases and images promote and reinforce one's goals. In self-healing, for example, patients repeatedly recite to themselves that they *are* getting healthier, then they visualize how their bodies' defense mechanisms are already overcoming the disease. With such verbal and mental affirmations, the mind can create the internal biochemical realities necessary for winning the fight.

Zen masters, business wizards, karate experts, leading-edge scientists, Hindu fakirs, and Olympic pole-vaulters all use a similar technique to achieve extraordinary feats. They've learned to mentally create their futures, rather than simply to suffer through them.

Positive affirmations and guided visualizations require extreme concentration and intense meditation, but the results (kicking a smoking habit, overcoming the symptoms of a bad cold, improving one's relationship and performance with a lover, making good money without sacrificing one's life-style) are more than worth the effort. Once you've begun seeing yourself with a positive mind-set, you'll experience a fresh sense of control over your future.

"So you would be the bold mouse?" Master Hui asked as Mount Tang's outline grew dim in the spreading dusk. "But what about the swift falcon perched near the field? Would you not worry that in your boldness you might lose your life?"

"Not me," replied Shen Ti. "Fear would not paralyze me. Knowledge of the falcon would simply force me to become stronger and faster."

Home is where the work is. Four years ago Paul and Sarah Edwards (Sierra Madre, CA) maneuvered their lives into a new and exciting arena. Paul, a lawyer by training, and Sarah, a psychotherapist, now make a living by providing people with the practical skills and management tools they need to work at home. Their products include books (most recently *Working from Home*) and cassettes, and even an online forum via CompuServe. More than 2,000 people regularly "teleconference" with them via computers, discussing and solving isolation and other problems associated with home-based businesses.

Why did Paul and Sarah leave safe careers in law and therapy? "We were looking for a new purpose in our lives," Paul says. "We were looking for something that would enable us to steer our own ship. So we spent a lot of time exploring our own possibilities, doing research, defining, and redefining. We had to figure out what's happening in the world and then try to combine it with what we do well. Through this process we refocused our vision in a major way and have made a career, an industry, a livelihood out of helping people work at home." As the Techno Age trend of working at home continues to grow, the Edwards plan to be on the cutting edge, providing new and better tools for the home-based business community.

Phase 3: Define Your New Identity: From Being to Doing

Once you've made positive affirmations a daily habit, you can set about developing a sense of yourself independent of your schooling, your job, or the traditional mold in which society and your upbringing have stuck you. Because our society has always blurred the distinction between who people *are* and what they *do*, breaking the mold requires a dedicated effort. Many of our surnames (Baker, Smith, Shepherd, Farmer) come from a time when people were known by their trade, a time when identity and livelihood were inseparably intertwined. Although succeeding generations have broken that bond, people still find their identities shackled to their occupations. Suppose you attend a cocktail party where you know only a handful of the guests. When you find yourself chatting with an attractive stranger, the conversation might go something like this:

"How do you know Rebecca [the hostess]?"
"We work together."
"Oh, you're in insurance?"
"Yeah, what about you?"
"I'm a high school history teacher."

Now imagine a couple of SE's running into each other at the same party:

"How do you know Rebecca?"
"We work together."
"Oh, you're in insurance?"
"In a way. I work at Long Life so I can put enough money in the bank to support my efforts at designing an annuity tracking system on my home computer."
"You're a programmer?"
"Naw, I majored in history. How about you?"
"Funny coincidence. I teach history at Tri State, but I've been consulting for companies doing business in Saudi Arabia. I majored in Middle Eastern studies."

Notice the differences here. While the former conversation restricted itself to "being" (who the people *are* in terms of their workaday jobs), the latter drifted to skills and abilities outside conventional job descriptions, and even shed light on some important hopes and dreams.

SE's approach work as whole persons who happen to be filling out time sheets for someone else at the moment. Not only does this attitude enable them to keep all important parts of themselves in view but also *it makes it okay for them to fail* at any given undertaking. Bernard Tessler, who started a highly successful educational software and computer store called the Enchanted Village, comments: "I've learned not to take things personally. As a human being you tend to take everything personally. But as you get involved in business, you learn that people aren't judging you as a person when you make a good or bad deal—they're simply judging your ability to negotiate."

Brett Johnson, who started Crowd Corp., a lucrative company that supplies caps emblazoned with corporate logos, says, "I never ever think about failure. If you meet only half of your intended goals, you're way beyond what you started with. The failures are short-term—in the long run they strengthen you as a person. Failure is just part of the educational process."

And Dwight Platt offers this advice to those who are thinking of becoming their own boss: "The worst thing that could happen to you is that you'll fail. And if you fail, you're worth three times more than when you started. When you start again, you won't make the same mistakes—you can't really lose, getting into business for yourself."

These SE's discovered that if you remain conscious of *all* your important skills and goals, you'll never feel your full potential worth diminished by failure. Rather, you'll simply learn from your mistakes and attack a new endeavor with relish. On the other hand, if your whole being rides on a specific job, failure can devastate what may be an already undermined self-image.

Does this mean that you shouldn't get too close to your work, for fear of finding your whole self drowned in it? Absolutely not. As Robert Pirsig eloquently describes in *Zen and the Art of Motorcycle Maintenance*, good work happens when the distinctions between subject and object fade away so that the doer becomes one with his or her task. How, then, do you resolve the apparent paradox of becoming organically entwined with your work while at the same time maintaining a separate identity from it? The answer: keep your ego in its proper place.

"Suppose the bold mouse ventures into the field and the falcon attacks," said Master Hui. "Would not boldness cost the mouse its life?"

Shen Ti thought about this for some time and then said, "That depends. If the mouse felt overconfident about its strength and swiftness, it might lose its life. But if it tempered its confidence with proper caution, it might only lose a tail."

Success was in the bag. Elizabeth Andrews (Portland, ME) kept her ego where it belonged. Five years ago this new mother worried about the hazards that the icy, blustery Maine winter posed to her baby's health. To solve the problem, Andrews, who holds a B.A. in Education, designed and built a "Baby Bag Snowsuit®" (a sleeping bag with legs) to keep her child warm. She now mass-produces the garment, wholesaling it through her Baby Bag Company, which turned a $10,000 investment into gross annual sales of more than $400,000. She confesses: "There were times early on when failure would have been terribly crushing personally. But now I've realized that even if I don't make it, it doesn't mean anything about me as a successful business person. The market is the way it is. Regardless, the Baby Bag Company has been a real success for me because my skills in so many areas have increased. My marketability as an employee is much better than before. Even if this thing ended up on its face tomorrow, I wouldn't take it as a defeat."

Phase 4: Welcome Risks: They Teach You More Than the Safe Bets

If you have learned to accept failure as a lesson in the school of hard knocks rather than a threat to your identity, you can start working on risking higher and higher bets. Again, many people shy away from the gaming table because our society has conditioned them to see "risk" as a danger. Just pick up the nearest newspaper or newsmagazine and look at the countless advertisements proclaiming a product or investment to be "risk-free, with a nothing-to-lose, money-back guarantee." The "risk of war" threatens the human race with extinction, not wearing safety belts "risks" lives on our highways, and the mortality rate among new enterprises makes striking out on your own a "risky move."

But it's really the old falcon-and-mouse game again. Mother mouse and bitter experience may teach the young mouse to avoid taking risks, but the mouse that never risks scampering across the kitchen floor never captures the cheese. Of course, not even the falcon takes unnecessary risks. It would not likely attack a larger predator or leisurely dine in the presence of hungry foes.

Likewise, SE's don't take foolhardy risks. But they do bet their time, skills, and egos on their future in a controlled way; they take *calculated* risks. As a result, SE's view risks not just as opportunities for financial and personal rewards, but as opportunities to learn and grow. While reckless risk can threaten our economic lives, calculated risk provides opportunity for change and improvement. "The risks are absolutely worth it," says Lorraine Mecca, who put her savings on the line when she started what evolved into one of the nation's largest computer wholesale companies. "The personal growth is enormous, because you know you'll have given it your all." Another SE insists, "I never saw trying my idea as a risk, I saw it as the next logical step in getting me to where I want to be." Yet another recalls how starting his own business was an exciting challenge with little to lose: "If the risk hadn't been there, there'd have been less reason to work as hard as I did. And the payoff was well worth it."

"Would you chance your tail for a morsel of grain?" Shen Ti asked his teacher.

"That would depend on my degree of hunger," Master Hui replied. *"And you?"*

"Oh, yes," Shen Ti said. *"If I were hungry enough, a tail*

*would be a small price to pay for the opportunity to fill my stom-
ach."*

A *picture is worth a thousand words*. Merna Popper (Ma-
maroneck, NY) had built up a solid art dealership over fourteen
years, so she surprised her friends and family (and herself) when
she tossed it all away to start *Women's News,* a tabloid that focuses on business and social issues for working women. After two
years the publication's circulation has grown to an impressive
250,000 in Westchester County, New York, and 250,000 in Los
Angeles County, California.

In a climate where six out of ten new magazines fail in their
first year, Popper certainly did take a gigantic risk, even if she did
draw on her own communication, marketing, and management
skills, learned during her gallery days. Nevertheless, she went
ahead with her publishing plans because she had a dream she
couldn't give up, regardless of the dangers she faced trying to
make it come true: "I've learned to enjoy reasonable risks, to live
on the edge. Once you get used to it, it's so much more exciting. I
sometimes ask myself what I would like to do that's safer, but I
know anything that doesn't give me a nervous flutter in my stom-
ach just isn't right for me. I've come to see 'the comfort zone' as
the real danger in life, because it's really not comfort at all—it's
laziness!"

Phase 5: Accept an Imperfect World: It's the Only One You Have

Now let's assume you've faced your internal demons, created a positive mind-set, you're not afraid of failing, and you're
even willing to take calculated risks. Imagine breaking out of the
mold, starting a bold new venture or accepting a challenging
new job. What happens if you achieve your financial goals but
find that you've had to compromise some life-style goals along
the way? Should you despair? No! Should you pursue some other
project? Maybe, but before you do, you must realize you've
reached a milestone in your SE career and will eventually have to
accept the fact that your world will never give you everything
you want.

Life is full of compromises. Like risks, however, they come in different sizes. On the one hand lies the "sellout," when you simply give up and resign yourself to so-called "fate." On the other hand lies the blindly determined "settle for nothing less," when you refuse to give an inch. *Beneficial compromises* lie somewhere in the middle.

Let's examine typical compromises any SE will likely encounter. First and foremost, you might have to give up the security of a regular paycheck. You must weigh that risk, however, against the benefit of being able to set your own hours, the luxury of being able to live where you want, and the potential to make as much money as your creativity and ingenuity can win. How can you make a beneficial compromise? Start out with a cushion in the bank, or, as Toni L. Goldfarb, who publishes *Medical Abstracts Newsletter*, recommends, "Try working on your idea while you still have your job. It might mean extra hours in the mornings, evenings, and weekends, but it's an excellent way to find out if you really want to make the move." Many SE's start off gradually, reducing their full-time work commitment as success comes their way. And some break away from corporations and start off by consulting to their old employer. Others let their current employer finance a new venture. Doing so may mean delaying the gratification of being strictly on your own, but it may also let you keep your peace of mind.

The next major compromise involves giving up a comfortable work environment. You'll probably begin by working in your kitchen, living room, or basement, and at first you'll miss the camaraderie of coworkers and friends. You might also find it hard to separate work from the rest of your life, since you'll almost be living on top of it. But you'll weigh these problems against the convenience of working at home, the relief from commuting, the reduced cost of child care, and the increased time you can spend with your family. Where are the beneficial compromises? Turn perfunctory lunches into meaningful social occasions, as journalist-turned-herb-grower Paula Winchester did: "I was afraid I wouldn't see anybody after I left to start a business from my house. But as soon as I realized that I could go out and schedule lunch hours with people of my choosing, I turned in my resignation!"

Other beneficial compromises could include: confining your

project to one room as far away from your living space as possible; building a nonwork change of pace into your daily schedule; convening meetings away from home; exercising over the lunch hour; or engaging in a favorite hobby in a different room from where you work. Michael Snell, who works out of his home, jogs from 11:30 to 12:30, eats lunch away from his office every day (at a luncheon meeting or picnic in the park), and fishes a nearby stream most evenings. Says Snell, "I've found I have to force a break in the routine, or I get cabin fever. But it beats hell out of commuting an hour into Manhattan to punch some other guy's time clock."

Finally, you'll lose the luxury of letting the buck stop on someone else's desk. Most people find the prospect of being responsible for everything down to the paper clips and pencil sharpener unnerving at first, but you can balance such trivial pursuits with the knowledge that you're learning new ways to apply old skills, gaining new skills, and sharpening your creative problem-solving and decision-making abilities. At the very least, you'll end up employable at a higher level than you are now. And that is the SE's "Golden Parachute." As Jack Rochester sums it up, "If you have to wind down your own enterprise and go to work for someone else, you might not come in as president. But you'll get there a lot faster than the person who doesn't know what it means to fly by the seat of the pants."

"What if the mouse loses more than its tail?" wondered Master Hui. "Suppose the falcon wounds it badly?"

Shen Ti did not hesitate with his answer. "Why, the smart mouse would go and find a field where the falcons are slower."

They dance to their own tune. "We were plain old burnt out," says Linda Gregg (New York, NY) about herself and her partner, Laurel Gruenwald. The two women had worked strenuously as dance therapists until they felt exhausted trying to turn their esoteric skills into hard cash. So they designed a kit to teach children about their bodies. At first they tried to produce the kit, but dropped the idea after looking into the development and marketing costs. Aware of the Techno Age romance between Americans and computers, they taught themselves a programming language and turned their kit into a software package called Body Basics.

Body Basics was a unique and interesting product, but it took an offshoot of that endeavor to throw Gregg and Gruenwald into the national limelight. When they ran into resistance to Body Basics from mothers who didn't understand or feared computers, the two SE's started Interpersonal Software, organizing Tupperware-like computer education parties for homemakers. Women clients felt comfortable asking basic questions in the company of their computer-phobic friends, and they flocked to the parties in droves.

Overnight success? Hardly. As Gregg admits, "Our friends didn't understand what we were doing, and they didn't take us very seriously. Some thought we were crazy! We were used to having a flow of people interested in our work and supportive of our efforts. All of a sudden we just had each other to stare at." Gregg and Gruenwald used their "isolation" period as a beneficial compromise, a time when they could learn new skills and build up a thriving business.

Phase 6: Trust Your Intuition: It Knows More Than You Think

Unlike the first five phases, this one occurs quite naturally once you've developed a positive mind-set and the right attitudes about failure, risk, and our imperfect world. At that point you'll find it easy to start listening to your gut feelings. More than anything else, SE's trust their survival instincts and their inner knowledge of strengths and limitations. When a project feels right, they don't fret and fuss; instead, they let their free spirits speak. Go with your own free spirit, trust it, let it guide you.

"How could you judge the falcon's speed unless you tested it by venturing into the field?" Shen Ti asked.

"Some knowledge comes from the heart," answered the Master. "The wise mouse trusts its instincts and the lessons experience has taught it."

Shen Ti thought about these words as Mount Tang blended into the darkness of the sky.

The sweet poetics of success. Bobbi Wolf (Merion, PA) has written poetry since she was a child. She recalls that whenever she had a thank-you card to write, she did it poetically. But could a childhood talent turn into a lucrative enterprise? Needing to stay home to care for a severely handicapped child, but yearning to use her creative skills in a business of her own, Wolf founded Poemetrics, a custom poetry-writing service that offers tailor-made poems for invitations, greeting cards, and announcements.

At first, Wolf charged three dollars per poem. After taking a small-business-development class at the University of Pennsylvania and consulting with the Small Business Association, she learned the marketing and management techniques needed to make her business fly. She then mastered the art of calligraphy and gradually raised her rate per poem to twenty dollars. Wolf comments that even though poetry had always been an integral part of her life, it took time to realize the treasure she had been polishing. "When something comes so naturally to you, it's often hard to realize that you can make a living from it. It really never dawned on me that I was living with a very marketable skill. Then one day it hit—this is it!"

ADDITIONAL TECHNIQUES FOR NURTURING A POSITIVE MIND-SET

A positive mind-set may take time and effort to achieve, but it requires even more to maintain it. Sometimes you'll enjoy a day of positive attitudes followed by two nightmarish days of negative thoughts. Given the fact that you're trying to undo many years of negative conditioning, that's to be expected. But don't despair. If you keep practicing the principles of positive mind-set until they become ingrained habits, you'll be able to fight off moments of desperation. Veteran SE's claim that the most important gift you can give yourself during this nurturing period is self-forgiveness, again and again and again. In addition, they recommend complementing your mind-set efforts by keeping your body in the best possible shape, and by controlling harmful "distresses" that inevitably accompany major changes in your life.

THE MIND-BODY CONNECTION

Since mind and body function inseparably, SE's strive to maintain harmony by keeping themselves in good physical shape. Only a strong body can survive the pressures of creating a positive mind-set and struggling for success. Not surprisingly, the most accomplished SE's run, bicycle, play racquetball, swim, or work out with Nautilus equipment. Such activities not only keep their bodies fit but also provide a necessary change of pace from the mental world that forms so much a part of the SE's daily life. Regular exercise also offers a useful fringe benefit: a strenuous exercise routine often reaches a point that one feels so relaxed or naturally "high" that solutions to previously unsolvable problems magically appear.

For example, Craig Hickman, a young executive of a dynamic private corporation, plays a vigorous game of racquetball every day and looks forward to what he calls the "finesse shot," a tactic that demands patiently waiting a few split seconds before returning the ball. While most players slam the ball at shoulder level, the finesse player waits until it almost strikes the floor, thus robbing an opponent of valuable response time. According to Hickman, the moment he plays the finesse shot a mental window opens up, letting him see creative solutions to pesky problems that may have been bothering him all day. He attributes some of his off-court success to the lessons of patience his finesse shots have taught him.

Others get the same results from "runner's high," the mental-physical harmony of martial arts, or the soothing effects of aerobic dancing. One SE's window opens midway through a daily bicycle workout that follows a twenty-mile bike path along the Charles River in Cambridge and Boston. Halfway through the routine he crosses the Massachusetts Avenue Bridge over the river and imagines the skyline along the riverbanks as his fixed set of ideas, the river flowing beneath him as a stream of new and creative ideas. The bridge itself represents a higher consciousness. Later in the day, whenever he encounters a problem, he visualizes the bridge: "When I let the thinking flow, the solutions flow."

TURNING DOWN INTERNAL NOISE: THE SE STRESS-REDUCTION PROGRAM

As we discussed earlier, a positive mind-set will naturally reduce the stress associated with the fear of failure and risk. Regardless of your positive attitudes, however, you cannot avoid the simple fact that making changes in your life produces stress. While this book cannot offer a complete course on stress reduction, it does suggest a few easy tricks that will help you deal with basic stresses that most SE's encounter (see also SE Library, Section VI, for selected readings on stress reduction).

Rule 1: Take Off One Hat Before You Put On Another.
SE's concentrate on compartmentalizing their lives in such a way that they can gain full pleasure and relaxation from their many activities. For example:

Make your meals pleasurable experiences, never allowing business worries to interfere with your diet. If you attend business meals, remember that you can gain more from forging a relaxed personal relationship than from negotiating a contract commitment. A good contract will often follow on the heels of a good friendship.

Let exercise be exercise—do it for the pure joy of it (insights may coincidentally pop up when you're thinking about something else, like your breathing or heartbeat). Susan Hauser has made pure exercise an important part of her basic routine. Says Hauser, "I run and do aerobics to burn off steam. I also love dancing, so lots of times when we go out to a business dinner, we go dancing afterward. It's not only a way to unwind, but it puts the dinner in proper perspective."

Finally, build focused friendship, family, and personal time into your hectic schedule. Marilyn Dashe, cofounder of a technical writing firm, recommends keeping a sharp boundary between family and work time. "I can keep the pressure off because I have a life outside of work. The minute my kids are home at the end of the day, I shift into school projects or some other activity that revolves around family members. I have two very active but very separate lives. I really think it helps keep everyone, including myself, happy."

Rule 2: Meditate or Carry Out Some Mental-Relaxation Technique.

Learn any of a number of simple and effective meditation techniques (see SE Library, Section VI). Many SE's find that meditation once or twice a day keeps their mental windows clean. When Michael Silva became CEO of Bennett Enterprises in Salt Lake City at the age of twenty-nine, employees of the troubled hundred-year-old $100,000,000-a-year firm expected dramatic changes; but Michael went to Hawaii for two months and sat on the beach. "I did nothing," he says. "But I meditated on the job ahead, and when I came back to Salt Lake I was able to turn a three-million-dollar loss into a million-dollar profit in one year."

Rule 3: Cultivate a Keen Sense of Humor.

Laughter, as the old saying goes, is the best medicine. Watch funny movies, read Woody Allen books, ask your friends and clients to tell you jokes. Whenever you experience a maddening or stressful event, step back from it, trying to think of it as an opportunity for a slapstick routine in a Three Stooges movie. Like a glass of water, any situation can be half serious or half funny. Always look for the half funny in your zany world. Software entrepreneur Martin Dean claims that his sense of humor helps him effectively control stress: "The company doesn't think of me as a very serious chairman of the board, but that's okay, it keeps me loose."

Here are two other techniques for using humor as a pressure relief: 1) Whenever you get into an uncomfortable interaction with clients, customers, or partners, just imagine that everyone involved has nothing on but underwear. That instantly diffuses the situation, so you can think more calmly and clearly. 2) At the end of a stressful or frustrating project write a parody of it. If told properly, wouldn't the story make someone smile?

Rule 4: Take as Many Vacations as You Can.

Vacations don't have to be major expeditions—even a week-

end or day trip will help you clear your head. Even the most
energetic SE needs time for a battery-recharging. SE Jed Roth,
who runs a unique and highly successful professional car-care
service, makes it a regular habit to escape his work environment:
"To reduce pressure, I travel. I hop on a plane and travel for three
hours in any direction. Maybe it's a jaunt out to Colorado for
some horseback riding in the Rockies, maybe it's a swing down to
the Florida Keys. I think when you're committed to something
that takes most of your mental and physical energy, coming
home doesn't get you away from it enough. You never forget
about it. So to clear my mind I go away for a fresh look at where
I'm heading."

Rule 5: Improve Yourself.

Don't let a week go by without adding at least one satisfying
improvement to your diet, exercise program, love relationships,
or personal appearance. Cut out another grain of salt, run a bit
harder or faster, refine your communication with your spouse or
lover, style your hair a little differently. Buy yourself gifts. And
not just practical items—give yourself toys that add a touch of
laughter and fun to your life.

Rule 6: Never Forget You're an SE.

Recite your mantra of success daily. Visualize yourself as the
financially secure person you can be, enjoying the life-style of
your dreams. Make your every waking and sleeping moment a
self-fulfilling prophecy of success. Trust your inner guide.

EXERCISE 2: MIND GAMES

The two games in this exercise will help you reinforce your
positive mind-set. They also lay the groundwork for the practical
applications of that mindset to a penetrating self-analysis.

Game 1: Lightning Bolt
   a. Think about the most important ability or skill that en-
      ables you to earn a living.
   b. Now imagine that a lightning bolt has erased the part of
      your brain controlling your special ability. You can never

use your skill again. What other income-generating skills could you dredge up from your repertoire of capabilities? Describe how you would set about immediately cultivating and marketing them.

c. Repeat step b, but this time imagine that the lightning bolt has destroyed all but one skill, a skill at which you consider yourself to have little aptitude. Can you use it to construct a scenario for success?

Game 2: Mental Versatility

a. Imagine yourself stranded on a desert island, completely naked, with nothing but a ball-point pen. How many survival scenarios, based on the pen, can you visualize? Here's one to contemplate:

1. You start off using the pen to stab jungle frogs and pry snails out of their shells.

2. Later on you discover poisonous mushrooms, and fashion poison darts to kill wild pigs. You disassemble the pen and use it as a blowgun.

3. To your dismay, you discover that unruly headhunters inhabit the far side of the island. At first you try to pretend you're one of them. You insert the pen cap through your nose to simulate a bone ornament and place the end plug in your navel as a sign of power. Unfortunately, this tribe does not wear such decorations, and your gesture of social solidarity doesn't work. They chase you out of their village, waving barbecue tongs and skewers. At various points along the chase you stick one end of the pen in your ear and the other to the ground. The pen then becomes a stethoscope enabling you to hear the otherwise inaudible footsteps of your hungry enemies.

4. Despite your superior technology, the headhunters steadily close the gap between you and their kettle. You dive into a pool and use the pen as a snorkel, and pray they'll mistake it for a bamboo reed.

5. Unfortunately, your bright blue "reed" is a dead giveaway, and you're summarily hauled out of the pool and strung like a wild boar over the open fire. Suddenly the chief's daughter chokes on an appetizer of

raw fish. You wriggle free of your ropes, grab the princess, and, as you once saw in a World War II movie, perform a tracheotomy with the pen, miraculously saving her life. The grateful chief gives you his daughter's hand in marriage, and you live like royalty for the rest of your life. (Women can alter the scenario to save the chief's son.)

b. Extend or change the scenarios to include at least five other uses for the ball-point pen.

c. Now perform the same exercise with one of your special skills or abilities. Break it up into components, as we did with the pen, and write down as many scenarios in which you can use your present skills to achieve your economic and life-style goals.

3

SELF-RECONNAISSANCE: SURVEYING YOUR HIDDEN ENTREPRENEURIAL TALENTS

By early autumn, the foliage in the valley transformed the landscape into a patchwork of brilliant color. Intoxicated by the splendid scenery around him, Master Hui assembled his students in a grove of golden ginkgo trees for a lecture on appearance versus reality.

"Everything in the cosmos has its own Tao, its unique Way," the Master explained. *"But one must go beyond appearances to see it." The Master then handed a golden ginkgo leaf to each student, asking for someone to explain how the leaves illustrated this idea.*

Disciple Shen Ti cleared his throat and said, "Look at how the leaves around us have changed from summer's soft green flexibility to autumn's dry yellow brittleness. On the surface, the Way of the leaf may appear to have changed. But its Tao is still to adorn the tree."

"Please explain," Master Hui said with a playful twinkle in his eyes, "how leaves adorn the tree if in winter they lie withered on the ground."

"They may have fallen," Shen Ti exclaimed as he tossed a handful of leaves in the air, "but by lying on the ground they

adorn the tree in a different way, by letting us see the grace and beauty of the tree's limbs!"

IT'S NINE A.M.: DO YOU KNOW YOUR TAO?

If you're like most people, by nine o'clock in the morning you're either getting ready to dive into a busy agenda or already hard at work. And whether you're a student, a bricklayer, or a homemaker, you probably employ many more skills than you realize. A French student reads, researches, discusses, and writes about Voltaire; a bricklayer draws upon construction skills to build a wall; and a homemaker orchestrates a variety of home-management skills that help her meet the needs of her children and spouse. If you were to ask these people to display their abilities in résumés, you'd find a number of explicit, well-defined skills listed. But while such descriptions might be accurate, they would reveal only a small portion of each person's true talent.

All of us, regardless of our levels of education, current occupations, or personal interests and abilities, possess a reservoir of hidden skills we can tap for our income-generating projects. The student may not realize the value of his or her ability to synthesize a mass of facts into a clear abstract, the bricklayer may not have considered his flair for design an explicit skill, and the homemaker may never have considered the lucrative ways in which she could apply her management and accounting skills. In fact, as most Soft-Skilled Entrepreneurs have found, hidden rather than visible skills usually determine whether or not they achieve goals.

This chapter will help you discover, display, and turn your hidden skills into valuable entrepreneurial tools. By the time you finish, you'll have mastered the art of constructing a personal SE skill inventory that will make you a winner in the Techno Age. You'll also learn how to build a hardball résumé that transforms previously unimportant phrases into powerful statements that clearly demonstrate your competence as an employee or master of a new enterprise. At nine A.M. you'll begin work with your new passport to success, your true Tao.

CHARTING A COURSE THROUGH THE UNSEEN: YOUR TACIT-SKILL DIMENSION

Think about soaping yourself in the shower. You *know* all the movements necessary for a good lather, but you don't consciously focus on them while you're scrubbing away. If you did, you'd get so hung up on details that you'd never get the job done.

Such *unconscious knowing* arises from what philosopher Michael Polanyi calls the "tacit dimension," a collection of beliefs, assumptions, and concepts that guides us through the world. We can take Polanyi's idea a step further by identifying and capitalizing on our "tacit" skills, those hidden abilities that ultimately enable us to succeed at work and play. Whereas explicit or "formal" skills such as writing, bricklaying, and homemaking indicate our abilities to perform specific tasks, tacit skills, such as abstracting, designing, and synthesizing, apply to more general tasks. While you use formal skills to accomplish a certain job, you can adapt tacit skills to virtually any project you choose, discovering rich and exciting new possibilities for applying your energies.

To illustrate this concept, let's consider tacit skills inherent in the formal skill of manuscript editing. The best editors can always keep in mind the whole work while they fuss with individual words and sentences. But how many editors would emphasize "dealing with part/whole relationships" on their résumés? How many would realize that such an ability suggests a good editor would also be skilled at strategizing and forecasting? Essential to good editing, and important in many business settings, such talents are highly valued in the Techno Age, where change occurs so rapidly that people who can spot trends in isolated and individual developments will give their own or their employers' projects a competitive edge. Those who have professional editing skills therefore sit in an ideal position from which to start enterprises such as industry newsletters or consulting services that forecast changes and preferences in various sectors of the economy.

That's exactly what John Gantz did. Gantz is a co-founder of *TechStreet Journal*, a newsletter that provides timely information on the financial side of the computer industry. He developed his talents at International Data Corporation, where he worked as a writer and editor for several years. What made his new venture successful? Not a degree in computer science, not advanced training in finance, but the hard-won ability to gather and disseminate timely information to a targeted audience. John could just as well apply these skills to a newsletter on chinchilla ranching or hydroponic gardening, without formal training in either subject.

As we'll soon see, tacit skills such as strategizing and forecasting come less from formal training and experience than from the abilities we must all develop to succeed at the daily game of life. Always keep in mind that tacit skills hide behind every formal skill and that each tacit skill crosses and recrosses formal boundaries, a fact that explains why homemakers, teachers, and Ph.D.'s in philosophy can create smashing successes in areas they know nothing about, be it computers or chinchillas. All of us can discover tacit skills by carefully examining three common environments: school (learning and teaching), work (as an employee and a manager), and play (hobbies and natural talents). In an effort to raise tacit skills to a conscious and useful level, let's consider specific skills that each environment fosters.

A LITTLE LEARNING IS A DIVINE THING: TACIT SKILLS EVERY STUDENT ACQUIRES

Most of us learn more tacit skills from our education than we ever realize. Whether you completed high school, a two-year junior college, a Ph.D. program, or have done postdoctoral research on insect symbolism in Kafka, you've learned how to think creatively, locate and manage information, present information, and work with others.

These skills give you a tremendous edge in the business world and can actually turn a soft-skilled background to your advantage. Steve Lawlor, a computer information systems professor who joined the Techno Age by starting Span Software Systems, comments that "a liberal-arts major might even do better in business than a business major. You can learn the practical stuff along the way. But the ability to bring fresh ideas to an established industry is really the greatest asset of all." As a student, you learn to generate those fresh ideas from some of the most seemingly mundane courses.

Consider, for example, what goes into preparing for a history exam. On a formal-skill level, one reads and studies and takes notes. But on a tacit level, a good student also masters the art of *abstracting, summarizing,* and *organizing* study materials; *evaluating* and *ranking* the most important ones; *psyching out* the teacher's exam style and *predicting* what will likely appear on the test; *allocating* enough time to study all the topics; and, most important, *managing* the available time while preparing for and taking the exam. As you can see, at least nine tacit skills are hiding behind the formal skills associated with exam preparation.

Every student has to write papers to fulfill course requirements. Before doing so, he or she uses a formal skill known as "researching," which also conceals a variety of tacit skills, including: *formulating* and *coordinating* a search strategy; *locating* and *retrieving* the research materials; *organizing* and *analyzing* the materials; *extracting* the key sections; and *documenting* sources. Chalk up eight more tacit skills! Can you imagine ways in which an SE might employ them to launch a project? Chris O'Donnell did. O'Donnell, an independent film and video sound recordist, recalls how his schooling made it possible to get his service off the ground: "When I was first looking for clients, I had to go to the library and find all the institutions and organizations pertinent to my field. Then I actually had to *go* to these places and weasel specific information out of them. There's no doubt that my college researching experience gave me the knowledge and confidence to do this."

After completing your research, you write your paper. And writing, of course, involves a storehouse of tacit skills, such as *outlining* and *maintaining a logical flow* of ideas; *presenting, describing,* and *characterizing* events, places, ideas, and people; *synthesizing* and *integrating the ideas of others; theorizing, concluding,* and *projecting* from your research materials; and *packaging* the paper attractively. Voilà! Eleven more tacit skills.

Peter Kinder, lawyer turned writer, and co-author of *Ethical Investing,* notes that "Writing is really a hybrid of time management and organization, and can teach the entrepreneur a lot. Say you have an opportunity that won't wait for you. You have to master the field, apply whatever techniques you use, and conquer it in a defined space of time. You don't have the luxury of waiting for it to hatch—you have to make it hatch. It's the same with a paper, an article, or a book; you have to move within the time frame you've been given and be ready to pounce on the next assignment."

Since the tacit skills underlying formally learned skills enable you to get things done, let's call them "logistical tacit skills." Such action-oriented skills form a major but by no means exclusive part of a good learner's abilities. So we must add "interpersonal tacit skills." Whereas a student's logistical tacit skills accumulate from preparing for exams, researching topics, and writing papers, interpersonal tacit skills come from immersion in the learning environment. For example, classroom or seminar participation teaches one a great deal about *sharing* information with others, *eliciting* information from others, and *cooperating* with others to achieve higher goals than a lone individual can accomplish.

Such interpersonal tacit skills augment the Soft-Skilled Entrepreneur's arsenal, for as writer/entrepreneur Brian Smith points out, "All entrepreneurs eventually have to come face to face with interpersonal issues. Unless you're going to hide behind a mail-order business, you'll never make it as an entrepreneur."

Although we could continue breaking down the learning environment into countless logistical and interpersonal tacit skills, such an exhaustive catalog lies beyond the scope of this book. Equipped with these general principles, however, you should be able to profitably mine your own vein of educational experience.

The high-spirited Shen Ti strode through the grove of ginkgoes, kicking up a brightly colored storm of leaves. Suddenly he shouted, "Master Hui! I've just experienced the Tao of learning."

"And how would you describe it?" Master Hui eagerly asked.

"I see the Tao of learning as letting the knowledge of any one thing spread to your knowledge of all things."

Making a living from living history. While working on her Ph.D. in Architectural History, Pauline Chase-Harrell (Boston, MA) volunteered to serve as a liaison to work with the city on a 19th-century exhibit for Boston's Bicentennial Celebration. As a result of her outstanding performance, she landed a consulting job on the exhibit and, deciding that "work was more fun than study," put her thesis on indefinite hold. Her success with the bicentennial project led to a string of other consulting assignments, in which she managed exhibits, supervised historic preservation, and coordinated fund-raising for preservation efforts. These in turn led to her election as chairperson of a commission that oversees the preservation of the city's sites, securing her a reputation in the Boston area as an expert on "cultural resource management." Soon she joined forces with a woman who specialized in social, political, and economic impact statements and together they founded Boston Affiliates, Inc., which draws from a pool of free-lance specialists in archaeology, anthropology, transportation, and fund-raising to solve problems related to the preservation of historic sites and the restoration of old buildings. She also offers "cultural resource management surveys," which forecast how a particular project will affect the historic sites in a certain area.

The abstract and complex nature of Chase-Harrell's work makes her thankful for the tacit communication and analytical skills she learned as a student. "The most important things I learned from college," Chase-Harrell says, "were how to write clearly and organize materials in a logical way. Because of those skills I can put together a good proposal. That's vital, because proposals are the means by which we get and do business. Equally important, though, is the ability to clearly describe what we do; our work is complex, so there's a real need to explain ourselves to others. Again, it's being able to communicate that makes all the difference."

THOSE WHO TEACH, CAN DO: TACIT SKILLS EVERY TEACHER POSSESSES

The formal skills involved in teaching may disguise a number of powerful tacit skills. Think about preparing a lecture for novices on a complex subject. Somehow the teacher must *translate* difficult concepts so students can grasp them. That might seem like a basic aspect of teaching, but in the business world such translation skills have many applications. In fact, this may be the single most important skill you'll need to start, develop, and maintain an SE project.

Ann Dixon, for example, uses her translation skills to promote the Guilford Cheese Company. After twenty years of teaching, Dixon decided to devote herself full-time to a farmsteading enterprise. Together with her husband and sons, she developed the means to produce Verde-Monte cheese, now sold in specialty shops throughout New England. According to Dixon, "There are lots of situations, from sales meetings to public demos, where I've called up the resources I've learned as a teacher. I've learned not only to be poised and confident in front of a group of people but also to impart information as thoroughly as if I were standing in front of a high school literature class. I also know how to adjust the level of my presentation so that it meets the needs of my audience."

Successfully using translation skills you developed as a teacher involves a good many of the learning skills discussed in the previous section, though it draws on them from a different point of view. First you must *define* the objectives of the lecture and *formulate* a strategy for achieving your goals. Then you must *conceptualize* how the lecture fits in with the broader objectives of the course. You may find *outlining* an invaluable skill in all of these preliminary phases. To expand your outline, you must *locate, retrieve, rank*, and *evaluate* potential materials before you can set about *abstracting, summarizing*, and *organizing* them. Naturally, *allotting* the right amount of time for all your activities will strongly influence the results. Besides *developing* a coherent presentation, you must also *psych out* your students so you can determine the best way to *motivate* them and hold their attention. This will depend on *packaging* the materials in a creative and stimulating way.

Notice how sixteen logistical tacit skills have sprung from the formal "preparing lectures" skill. All good teachers use some or all of these tacit skills every day and can easily transfer them to the business world, be it a corporate job or an entrepreneurial endeavor. Ann Dixon says that whenever she gives a product presentation to cooking classes, "I organize it like any class lecture, preparing outlines, summaries, and other instructive handout materials." And Steve Lawlor remarks, "In business I can use my teaching techniques to communicate my ideas and aspirations in hopes that others will work toward them. I once gave my employees a thirty-minute lecture on what profit was and why it was so important. That lecture really paid off in terms of the progress of my company."

Effective teaching, though, takes more than effective preparation. A lecture's success will ultimately depend on delivery. First you'll need the confidence to speak in front of groups. Beyond that, the quality of your delivery will depend on *depicting* concepts in a lively way, *reinforcing* your audience's understanding of the materials through spontaneous remarks, *sensing* when you've lost or bored your students, and *managing* your delivery within the allotted time.

Finally, teachers develop interpersonal tacit skills from advising students and working with colleagues and administrators. To successfully guide students you must be good at *empathizing* and *nurturing*, while to work successfully with others in your department, you must be capable of *collaborating, cooperating,* and *sharing.*

Clearly, teachers can uncover a rich assortment of tacit skills for their educational experience, but they will often find dealing with information and people the most important when it comes to SE projects.

"And what of the Tao of teaching?" Shen Ti asked Master Hui.

"The Tao of teaching mirrors the Tao of learning. You know the yin and yang of learning, wherein the student who pliantly receives knowledge gains the power to act on that knowledge. In the same way, as teacher I learn as much as my students, for I must constantly clarify my knowledge before passing it on."

From classroom to boardroom. For Lorraine Mecca (Santa Ana, CA) it became evident after two years that teaching would never satisfy her life-style goals. So she took an entry-level clerical position with a component wholesaler. Within two years she had learned the ropes and had risen to the position of production coordinator in charge of processing almost all the firm's paperwork. Confident that her performance merited a raise, she invited her boss to lunch and popped the question. As Mecca recalls, "He resisted the idea, and it wasn't until I literally cried that he gave in. After that I decided that I would never cry for money again." To make good on her promise to herself, Mecca aimed for Techno Age stardom by starting her own computer wholesaling company. And she was willing to gamble every last penny on her own skills and dedication. Did it pay off? Handsomely. Today Micro D generates more than $100 million a year in gross sales.

Although Mecca left the classroom, she cherishes the skills she acquired from her stint as a teacher. Says Mecca: "In my own company, I'm primarily responsible for sales training. Working as a teacher gave me a lot of insights and practical experience in organizing training materials and evaluating skills advancement. My communications skills also come into play every day. Thinking logically as a communicator enables me to solve tough business problems; I just present a thesis and develop each point in a logical manner. I also think the experience of having talked in front of a classroom for two years has helped me feel confident about talking to my own staff of 180. When I present an idea, I'm not the least bit nervous that someone will shoot it down."

WORKING TOWARD A LIVING: TACIT SKILLS LEARNED ON THE JOB

Next to school, our jobs probably offer the richest source of new skills. At work you undoubtedly use both formal and tacit skills picked up in school, but you have probably had to sharpen those skills or learn new ones to succeed at a job. Sure, you might have learned how to set up a ledger in an accounting course, but your real knowledge of accounting will come from dealing with situations and problems the textbooks never teach. In short, at work you'll learn the tricks of the trade. Regardless of your occupation as a full- or part-time employee, you're in a position to benefit greatly from on-the-job training (OJT), which will serve you either by helping you advance in the corporation or by giving you the tools you need to start your own business.

SE's, constantly alert for logistical and interpersonal tacit skills, know how to make the most of OJT. If you've ever held a job somewhere for more than a day, you undoubtedly found yourself *interpreting* and *analyzing* instructions, *deciphering hidden agendas*, and *anticipating* the next assignment. You probably learned how to acquire the information necessary for *assigning priorities* to tasks and *strategizing* the best way to accomplish them. Then, as you gained your employer's trust, you probably received additional responsibility for *administering* and *managing resources*, and *training* other people. In short, you've picked up a number of tacit logistical skills.

If you've ever worked for someone else, you've gained another set of valuable tacit skills. Good managers provide good role models, teaching you the subtleties of productive work habits. Every SE interviewed for this book stresses the importance of being able to *meet deadlines, work under pressure,* and *give your best,* even through the most tedious and unpleasant tasks. These qualities can make or break an SE, because no matter how much you love your project, no matter how much you've dedicated yourself to its success, you'll be putting in long, hard hours, often on dull or repetitive aspects that will test your resolve. If you learned from those who managed you on the job, you'll be in a good position to manage yourself. Regina Collins-gru, founder of a word-processing service, notes that "typing is the least of the skills I carried over from my secretarial days. Much more important, when I started my business I knew how to juggle deadlines. I knew that deadlines can't always be met and that I had to be resourceful when a crisis arose. Also, none of the piddling little problems that crop up in my business are a bother to me, because I learned how to handle those kinds of things when I was working for other people. And I know how to go out and get the proper information when I need it."

Another important OJT skill comes from the art of networking (see Chapter 6). By building networks of friends, clients, suppliers, and fellow SE's, you can accomplish many times more than what you could as a solo player. To network successfully you need to be able to work with people on an equal-to-equal basis, an interpersonal tacit skill you can learn from almost any job. Whether you work for a three-man chimney-sweeping operation or a Fortune 500 firm, you never work in a vacuum. From working shoulder-to-shoulder with others, you've learned the value of *integrating* yourself into a team effort and *combining* talents in the spirit of cooperation. You probably also learned ways of *facilitating* objectives for your co-workers and superiors. In short, you learned the art of *giving* to and *taking* from those around you in a balanced way that helps the organization accomplish its goals.

As we saw earlier, SE's are highly adaptable creatures. Where do they learn to be quick-change artists and chameleons? On the job, where they've had to find ways of adapting their strong personalities and financial-life-style goals to an organization and its management. Most successful SE's have learned to accommodate to a wide variety of working habitats. Sure, many SE's, tired of being corporate serfs, eventually abandon conventional jobs, but they never forget that they can always handle a variety of situations.

SE Barbara Brabec, who turned a $1,000 investment into a $100,000-a-year publishing business, comments on an unexpected skill she picked up in a high school summer job: "I was chopping worms off ears of corn in the production line of a corn-canning factory, probably the worst job in my life. But it paid well, and taught me a lot about hard work, discipline, and the ability to *endure*. Throughout the day, a conveyer line of empty tin cans rattled and banged not three feet away from my head. In sheer desperation, I learned to tune out this noise because I couldn't stand it otherwise. The payoff, of course, is that absolutely nothing can distract me from my work because I simply won't allow it."

As the afternoon grew colder, Master Hui began leading his disciples home. On the way they passed a monastery, where monks with straw brooms busily swept the paths. "Can you describe the Tao of working?" Master Hui asked Shen Ti.

"Work, too, expresses yin and yang?" ventured Shen Ti.
"How so?"
"The monks' sweeping not only clears the path; the activity makes their muscles stronger."

Librarian turned P.R. expert turned SE. When Brenda Ellis (Cambridge, MA) signed on as the business librarian at the State Street Bank, she thought she had found her lifelong career. After two years, though, she became so fascinated with public relations that over the next six years she held virtually every P.R. and marketing-support job in the bank. One day she realized she faced only two options: no further advancement or out the door to greener pastures.

So Ellis went job hunting and soon secured a position as general manager of a small software company, which to everyone's surprise experienced severe reversals two years later. Unemployed, Ellis dredged up every formal and tacit skill she had to start her own enterprise, The Office At One Kendall Square, a cooperative office suite where traveling executives, itinerant consultants, and other Techno Age nomads can enjoy elite secretarial services and office equipment.

Looking back, Ellis finds that the skills she used at the bank really enabled her to get The Office going: "The most important thing my work has shown me is that almost anything you want to know *exists*, and you just have to figure out where to get it."

Of course the public-relations and marketing skills Ellis acquired at State Street came in handy too: "They gave me the confidence to make it work."

BEYOND THEORY Z: TACIT SKILLS LEARNED FROM MANAGING OTHERS

You don't need a fancy title to learn from managing others on the job. Vice-presidents may formally manage platoons of lieutenants, but experienced workers, free-lancers, and homemakers also take responsibility for managing people and the settings in which they work or live. Training someone to do your job after you leave involves management, as does directing the efforts of a colleague or assistant. Any successful manager develops a number of logistical tacit skills for ensuring that jobs get done well and on time. Such skills make a big difference to any SE project, for as one homemaker turned Soft-Skilled Entrepreneur comments, "If you can get your kids to eat what you want them to, you can certainly convince a bank to loan you the seed money you need for a business venture."

Much of a good manager's success depends on his or her ability to communicate clearly. So whether you're dealing with staff members, suppliers, or your family, you should learn how to *present your desires and instructions* clearly and unambiguously. Once you convey the right message, you draw on your skills of *guiding and facilitating others* to carry out your plan. Then, after *assessing the progress* that your people have made, you must be capable of *revising your goals* and *redirecting your energy* to meet the realities of a changing situation.

Management also provides valuable interpersonal tacit skills. If you're a good manager, you must *recognize and reconcile problems* between people. That means being capable of *arbitrating disputes* in an evenhanded way, *setting limits* and *establishing policies*. Your success at these tasks will largely depend on whether you're good at *creating and projecting an authority image*. If so, then you're probably capable of *motivating and stimulating those around you*. Recalls Warren Holland, creator of the Decipher puzzle, "I was managing people in the construction business. Now I'm managing the managers. I give them guidelines as to how I'd like things run, and we sit around and talk about how things are going. These kinds of techniques really let people grow and develop personally, and that's what a job should be all about."

Many SE's with managerial experience find that their logistical and interpersonal tacit skills enable them to easily start and sustain a project of their own. As Jan Williams, who founded a recording studio and record exchange, comments, "Being a manager really comes down to being a good problem solver. And problems galore are what you'll face when you start your own business, for at least the first year or so. But having that experience and orientation will cut it all down to 'business as usual.' So you're less likely to find yourself climbing the wall."

"You lead, and I'll follow," observed Shen Ti as he carefully set his foot where the Master had just stepped. "Tell me about the Tao of leading."

Master Hui smiled. "By following, one learns to lead; and by leading, as by teaching, one learns to follow."

She acted on her dreams. Throughout high school, Eleanore Parker (Dedham, MA) fantasized about working in the theater. The idea became squashed, though, when she enrolled in a teachers college that offered no majors but teaching. Then Parker's desire for theater work came to life again several years into her teaching career, when she organized a traveling children's theater troupe. Parker handled all the booking and made all the logistical arrangements, while her partner did the directing. The theater never made much money, but it gave her excellent experience.

Five years later, Parker had a baby and quit teaching. With time on her hands, she decided to expand her theatrical repertoire by organizing a traveling music revue. Eventually she established a 400-seat dinner theater in conjunction with a restaurant in New Hampshire and was suddenly responsible for everything: sales, publicity, and budgeting, as well as having to keep abreast of all the managerial details involved in running a theater. To her surprise, the theater began to make money: "It was my dream come true," says Parker. "I was working in the theater, commuting to New Hampshire. We got terrific press, and were usually filled to eighty percent of capacity."

But as quickly as it started, the restaurant collapsed, leaving Parker without a theater, without a staff, and without an income. Parker was devastated and demoralized; her dream had shattered. While looking through the want ads one day, she spotted an ad for a receptionist at a national lecture agency. She decided to look into it, hoping to bide her time as a receptionist until she found something better to do. "It turned out that they also needed a full-time booking agent. Because of all my theater experience, they hired me on the spot. I went home and cried. I needed a job very badly, but I really didn't want to work for someone else." Nevertheless, she took the job.

It took Parker another four years to quit her job at the lecture agency, but once she did, she knew she would never work for anyone else again. With a telephone, a typewriter, some letterhead stationery, and a few thousand dollars she'd borrowed from her father, Parker started a P.R. firm called Good News! "It was crazy," Parker remembers. "I not only had to learn how to run a business, I had to learn the business. I didn't have any formal P.R. experience. What I knew came from typing my former husband's reports. No P.R. firm would have ever hired me."

Although her experience as a producer seems relatively unrelated to her enterprise, she actually gained invaluable managerial and interpersonal skills in the theater. "A lot of P.R. involves dealing with the media," she says, "and I was entirely responsible for publicizing the dinner theater, including press releases every week and getting the local press down to see the shows. So the media don't intimidate me. Also, in the theater I was supervising more than thirty people at one time. So dealing with two or three part-time employees isn't all that threatening."

"But," says Parker with a laugh, "and you may be surprised to hear this, the most valuable skill of all has been my telephone skill. You know, spending a lot of time on the telephone and coming across well is a real art. It's the tool I use most in my office, and I think it's gotten me the most clients. So all that time booking performances and lecturers over the phone hasn't gone to waste." Good News! is rapidly growing, and Parker's clients range from gallery owners to computer companies. She proves that no experience is ever wasted.

PLAYING FOR KEEPS: TACIT SKILLS GLEANED FROM HOBBIES AND PERSONAL INTERESTS

Many of the best SE projects start off as hobbies, pet projects, or expressions of personal interests. Most people work at their hobbies in an unencumbered way—no deadline pressures, no one hanging over their shoulders, no performance expectations other than those they impose on themselves. Such an environment provides fertile ground in which creative ideas can flourish.

Many SE's tap hobbies and personal projects as profitable sources of logistical tacit skills. Whether you've learned to play a musical instrument, grow prize zucchini, or build a solar panel for your house, you've already become skilled at *figuring out or deciphering instructions*. And you've learned to *adapt and modify general ideas* to meet your own needs and style. Other logistical tacit skills that spring from hobbies include *managing time and resources* and *setting goals*. Most important, as the person "in charge" you also become a manager, using many of the tacit decision-making and interpersonal skills described earlier. Stanley Plog, a former psychologist who now runs a luxury car-rental service, remarks how his interests in music surprisingly turned into an excellent source of useful business skills. "Music gave me my greatest skills," Plog says. "I had my own band before college and I had to learn how to knock on doors and present myself. You also have to stay tasteful and entertaining but you mustn't look sloppy. What else? Music really gave me the confidence to stand up to the big guys and be myself."

If you love your hobby, why not transform it from an avocation to a vocation? Many SE's, often homemakers, become so absorbed in a personal project they don't realize it could easily blossom into a viable business. In the words of Nancy Thode, who consults to parents about overnight camps, "I'd been advising people for many years on an informal basis. Then it dawned on me one day I was doing a valuable service. So I decided that what I was doing was really a business, and here I am—owner of the Camp Advisory Service."

When they had arrived at Master Hui's dwelling, Shen Ti admired one of his teacher's paintings. "Your pastime must provide a welcome relief from the strain of teaching all day," Shen Ti said.

The Master shook his head. "Do you not see how my landscapes express my understanding of nature and the human condition? My pastime and my life are one."

A lifelong hobby becomes a full-time career. When Sherrill Boggs (Columbia City, IN) approached her fortieth birthday, she decided to realize a childhood dream: building a greenhouse for exotic plants. Her interest in horticulture had been sparked at age three, but its growth had been stunted during her years as a student and later as a salesperson. Finally, after saving enough money, she built a greenhouse attached to her garage. Within weeks the place overflowed with flowering plants, bushes, and vines. In order to solve a blooming overpopulation problem, Boggs began to sell her plants out of her home at Tupperware-like parties. When she realized that her job brought her one tenth the joy she got from her hobby, she decided to try to support herself by growing and selling plants. So after renting a small store, the green-thumbed entrepreneur set up shop. A month later, while chatting with a caterer who rented the space below hers, Boggs had a flashing brainstorm: if she and the caterer could join forces, they could offer a one-stop wedding service that would include all necessary catering and floral services. Why, they could even offer to handle invitations and tuxedo rentals. Her store, Anything Groes, has become a major hit in the Columbia City area, as Boggs continually adds new and exciting refinements. "It's not only answered a childhood dream," she says, "but it's been a rare opportunity to fulfill my creative and financial needs by doing something that really comes from the heart."

NOBODY DOES IT QUITE THE WAY YOU DO: TACIT SKILLS THAT COME FROM A PERSONAL FLAIR

Everyone displays unique attributes, skills, or talents, but somewhere along the line people tend to stifle certain inherent traits in an effort to conform to preestablished notions of the correct way to behave. Too few of us put our native flair to work in our careers. But when you ignore that flair, unfortunately, you fail to hone and sharpen traits that could bring you far more personal success than conformity ever provides. That's why SE's always strive to nurture their unique traits, creating custom-tailored niches for themselves within their present jobs or within projects of their own making. SE Robert Florzak did just that when he included in his public-relations consulting firm teaching executives how to run microcomputers: "I have the kind of mind that naturally loves learning," Florzak says. "So I've become flexible enough to do consulting in all sorts of fields. As a result I've gained expertise in everything from workmen's compensation to computer telecommunications."

Another entrepreneur, John Monroe, found a way to turn his natural problem-solving ability into a thriving pursuit. Since World War II, Monroe has been a professional problem solver, as a professor of geology at Baylor University and as a consultant to the U.S. government. He also holds numerous patents for lasers and other optical devices. Two years ago, he was visiting a technical school that taught automotive repair, and noticed that there were no teaching devices to help students diagnose engine problems on the basis of sound. At the same time, he knew that car noises provided rich clues into the nature of mechanical problems. The solution? Cassette recordings of car sounds, complete with narratives explaining their significance. Monroe set up Audio Diagnostics to produce, market, and distribute the tapes, which caught on so well that they're now being used at technical schools throughout the country. He's also created a simplified version for do-it-yourself mechanics.

For Monroe, Audio Diagnostics is just another problem-solving exercise. "Society has no voids," Monroe speculates. "When something appears to be missing, you just have to work at finding the piece that fits in. That's how I solve any technical problem."

As Florzak and Monroe show, one should never lose sight of the unique natural abilities that form their core of the Tao. Such innate talents ultimately enable one to conceive and shape projects that bring the most lasting success and satisfaction.

☯

Before bidding his disciples farewell, Master Hui asked, "Can anyone explain how each of you follows the Tao of the disciple, but each looks and acts so differently?"

Shen Ti spoke for the group. "I use my learning to write poems, while Wei Ming uses his to prepare for military service.

In this way we may all gain the same understanding, but each of us will use it for different purposes."

Improving on chip technology. "All I did was take the basic chocolate chip cookie and give it my personality, add a few more chips, give it a little coconut, and then bake it the way I like it to taste," says Wally Amos (Honolulu, HI), creator of the Famous Amos chocolate chip cookie. Amos, a former show-business promoter, was sitting in his office one day when a client walked in with a bag of delicious homemade cookies—so good he found it hard to believe the recipe came from the back of a plain old package of Nestlé's chocolate chips. Amos began baking his own homemade cookies and bringing them to business meetings, letting them work their chocolate charm on his clients. He also dealt them out to friends and began fancifully thinking about selling them. But fantasy turned into reality when B. J. Gilmore, a friend at A & M Records, seriously suggested they go into business together.

Eureka! Amos turned a growing restlessness with show business into a surge of energy. With the help of a great network of friends whose palates had all been delighted by Amos's cookies at one time or another, he founded the world's first chocolate-chip-cookie store, the opening celebration of which drew an invited 1500 guests. Today you can find Amos's cookies throughout the world, and you'll even see him enshrined in the Business Americana collection of the Smithsonian's National Museum of American History.

What ultimately enabled Amos to elevate the chocolate chip cookie from a mundane munchable to a fast-selling trend? "Marketing flair," says Amos. "I refer to marketing as promotion, which is what I know best. Since I'd been promoting people for fourteen years, I just had to figure out a way to turn cookies into people. My concept was that chocolate chip cookies are superstars. It was a winning proposition."

Amos signed on "The Cookie" as if it were any other client, possibly becoming the first personal manager for a bakery product. As Wally Amos discovered, taking a creative approach to an old idea can open the window to success. "Every recipe is the same," he says. "It's just the individual that makes them better."

UNCOVERING YOUR OWN STOREHOUSE OF TACIT SKILLS

By this point you should have gotten a good sense of how to go about identifying and making more explicit all the tacit skills you acquired from school, work, and play. Now that you've seen the forest and have a sharp ax in hand, it's time to start chopping your own trees. Take a shot at the following two exercises— they'll give you some handy timber for building an SE résumé that will enable you to play hardball with even the softest of skills.

EXERCISE 3.1: COMPILING A PERSONAL SKILL INVENTORY

As you've seen from reading this chapter, even the most seemingly mundane activities can harbor valuable tacit skills. That's why a personal skill inventory takes *everything* into account.

Review your student days, your past and present jobs, and your personal talents, hobbies, and interests. Look for skill-laden activities and events like those discussed throughout the chapter. The following checklist will give you some starting points—add to or expand the categories to reflect your own particular situation.

PERSONAL SKILL INVENTORY

ENVIRONMENT I: EDUCATION

SKILL SOURCE	FORMAL SKILL	TACIT SKILL(S)

A. Learning
1. Lecture courses
2. Seminars
3. Independent studies
4. Honor papers/ presentations
5. Master's thesis
6. Doctoral thesis
7. Academic fieldwork
8. Work in clubs/ associations/fraternaties/sororities
9. Political/student organizing
10. Volunteer work

B. Teaching (not necessarily in a classroom)
1. Lecture courses
2. Seminars
3. Independent studies
4. Arranging field studies
5. Tutoring
6. Career advising
7. Curriculum development and revision
8. Work in professional associations

ENVIRONMENT II: WORKING

SKILL SOURCE	FORMAL SKILL	TACIT SKILL(S)
1. Clerical		
2. Administrative		
3. Managerial (people)		
4. Managerial (projects)		
5. Work in unions/trade/ professional associations		
6. Proposal writing		
7. Negotiating changes in work environment/ salary		
8. Reviewing and assessing job performance		
9. Training new staff members		
10. Writing job descriptions		

ENVIRONMENT III: PLAY

SKILL SOURCE	FORMAL SKILL	TACIT SKILL(S)
1. Visual arts		
2. Music		
3. Performing Arts		
4. Crafts		
5. Hobbies/collections		
6. Volunteer work with community/		

nonprofit/political/
school/religious
organizations
7. Affiliation with clubs/
associations
8. Sports

EXERCISE 3.2: WRITING A HARDBALL RÉSUMÉ

What is a "résumé"? According to Webster's Third, it is a "summing up, especially a brief account of one's education and professional experiences." For the SE, a résumé is more. It is a work of art that creatively but accurately makes all the SE's tacit skills explicit and marketable. SE's don't lie on their résumés, they simply tell the whole truth.

Before you begin to write your résumé, remember the difference between illustrating the depth of your experience and *padding* your résumé. There is never a need to fluff up your experience if you truly understand its value; besides, a good résumé reader can see right through such an attempt. There is a saying among college admissions officers that goes: "The *thicker* the packet, the *thicker* the kid." Words and paper don't make a good candidate for anything. Hardball players are fit and trim.

In order to keep their résumés in top shape, many SE's keep more than one around—one might be for "business," another for "teaching/instruction." Each contains some elements that are the focus of the other, but not in as substantial a form. Other SE's keep one big résumé around with *all* of their skills and experiences listed. Then they cut and paste appropriate material into place.

Examine the following assortment of résumé entries. Notice how the SE versions use the same facts as the conventional ones, but also reveal the person's full capabilities. That means a prospective employer or client won't have to guess about what a person really can do—it will *all* be there in black and white. With these examples in mind, haul out your old résumé, dust it off, and rewrite it with the tacit skills you discovered in Exercise 3.1. Then get ready for a game of hardball.

CONVENTIONAL ENTRY	SE VERSION
Public Relations Officer University of Rochester. Wrote press releases about faculty research. Sent to newspapers and magazines. Served on Community Outreach Committee.	*Public Relations Officer* University of Rochester. Located and analyzed materials for articles about faculty research. Interviewed faculty. Wrote press releases and communicated regularly with media. Special project: Directed telephone survey of local residents proving need for community health care instruction by members of university staff.
Travel Agent Colonial Travel Agency. Booked airline and hotel reservations, arranged chartered packages, provided long-distance customer assistance. Promoted to Customer Assistance Manager.	*Travel Agent* Colonial Travel Agency. Analyzed most economical air routes for clients. Researched and evaluated components for charter packages. Special project: Arranged emergency accommodations when tour bus broke down 150 miles from Bogotá, Colombia. Subsequently promoted to Customer Assistance Manager.

Placement Officer
Manning Personnel Agency.
Called local businesses to see
if they needed additional personnel. Also recruited individuals seeking employment.

Placement Officer
Manning Personnel Agency.
Evaluated and placed qualified candidates in various
positions with local businesses.

Special project: Designed one-
page survey to help businesses
assess their employment
needs.

Secretary
Alpha Insurance.
Typed, filed, answered
phones, ordered supplies, ran
postage and copy machines.

Secretary
Alpha Insurance.
Provided clerical and communication support to principals;
maintained inventory; moni-
tored operation and service of
office equipment.

Special project: Set up employee newsletter and bulletin
board for 60-person support
staff.

Hobbies: Gardening, travel.

Personal Interests:
Gardening
22 years. Recently set up
community garden in neighborhood back lot.

Travel
I prefer to travel on foot,
bicycle, or by train in order
to get the fullest experience of
other cultures. Traveled extensively in South America, Europe, and northeastern
United States.

4
RIDING THE TECHNO AGE CURRENTS: HOW TO DEVELOP IDEAS INTO PROJECTS

Cold winds began blowing across the valley soon after the last of the autumn leaves had fallen to the ground. With his students gathered around his stove, Master Hui decided to turn their thoughts inward.

"To know a thing is to have an idea of its li, its essential pattern," the Master said as he peered into the glowing stove. "But essences often escape our attention. What, for instance, is the li of fire? The flames dance and change each moment. Only through deep meditation on the fundamental nature of fire can one see through its elusive appearance."

After a moment of silence, Shen Ti asked the Master to hold out his hand. Then he reached into the stove with a poker to fish out a fiery ember, which, to the horror of everyone, seemed about to drop onto the Master's palm. Shen Ti, though, did not let it fall. "The flames may wildly dart about and confuse your understanding," he said, "but one may experience their li quite easily. You can surely feel heat without pondering fire's essence for many days."

Master Hui laughed and withdrew his hand. "When it comes to knowing, Shen Ti, the hand may be quicker than the mind. But you may lose some skin."

"Perhaps," his disciple replied, "but once burned, once en-lightened."

OUT OF THE FIRE AND INTO THE PAN

At one time or another, every SE gets burned testing an idea. Some suffer a mild scorching, like taking a clever shortcut to an appointment, only to find themselves sweating behind the steering wheel in the middle of a marathon traffic jam. Others suffer third-degree burns after investing their life savings in Ramasheesh Airlines the day before Treasury agents nab the company's officers for tax evasion and padlock the hangar.

Whatever the case, and despite the outcome, SE's salve their wounds with the knowledge that they have gained valuable lessons from their experiences. The world of Soft-Skilled entrepreneurship is like Master Hui's stove: while you might occasionally singe your nose with a hot idea, you follow the maxim "Once burned, twice *smart*," always pursuing new ideas, but learning to thoroughly evaluate them before you strike your match.

In this chapter, you'll find a four-part plan for helping you devise and develop good SE project ideas. First you'll learn about the sorts of ideas most likely to succeed in the Techno Age. Next you'll acquire the ability to listen for the *clicks!* that help you spot profitable new ones. With your hot ideas in hand, you'll proceed to research their viability and determine whether the timing is right. In the end you'll be able to write an SE proposal for converting your hot idea into cold, hard cash.

SOFT-SKILLED STRATEGY FOR SUCCESS

Step 1: Learning to Think in Techno Age Terms

The case studies throughout this book illustrate the fact that good Techno Age ideas share many common traits, or "Universal Project Themes." If you look closely, you'll see that most of the projects in this book play variations on the following themes, which serve as guidelines for conceiving and developing ideas.

Project Theme I: Help people save time. This theme spawns moneymaking projects related to business and life-style management in the Techno Age. It is quite popular among SE's, as it often requires little or no start-up capital. Some SE's, for example, make a living as "purchasing agents" by standing in lines for other people who want to buy theater or movie tickets or who need to pay parking tickets and other fines in crowded metropolitan areas. All it requires is a little low-cost advertising and a good pair of shoes. A variation on this theme is to bring stores or services to people's doorsteps. David Kolodziej exemplifies this approach with Entertainment to Go, a unique service that delivers video movies and dinners to its customers. Another variation has been perfected by Jed Roth, who saves luxury-car owners a trip to the car wash by picking up their autos and then returning them spotless, waxed, and buffed. The possibilities for such time-saving projects are almost limitless.

☯

"And what of time?" Master Hui asked disciple Shen Ti. *"How can you experience its essence?"*

"That is even easier than getting to know the li *of fire,"* Shen Ti answered. *"All you have to do is wait. . . ."*

☯

A **stitch in time.** "An hour of searching a data base by computer can be the equivalent of ten to twenty-five times faster than manual searching," Maureen Corcoran (Gainesville, FL) says. And she should know. Her business, Online Connection, is exclusively dedicated to the fine art of finding information by computer. (In computerese, "online" means that the computer "talks" on the telephone to electronic libraries or "data bases" around the country. Once the computer dials the data base, it can sort through vast amounts of information in mere seconds.)

Corcoran was first exposed to online data-base searches while working on her master's in Information Science degree. Before long, she became so fascinated by the growing use of computers in her field that she decided to become a computer whiz. Speaking from an enlightened Techno Age perspective, Corcoran says, "The librarian tries to see the structure in a problem, and then goes to a card catalog to try to solve it. Computers are a logical extension of this method because they have an internal structure of their own. I found that I was good at using them and that they're the perfect tool for finding information quickly and cheaply."

After receiving her M.S. degree, Corcoran took a job at the University of Florida in a business "outreach" center, using on-line techniques to do research for clients. Three years of online searches convinced Corcoran that she could sell her own high-tech information consulting service, so she set up Online Connection, investing a modest sum in a computer and the other gadgets needed to tap into data banks. Her fees support the company and provide her with the kind of life-style she wants. She comments that "clients are really buying my technical expertise. They know and trust my understanding of many different kinds of businesses and information sources. Most important, they know that my searches are complete and cost-effective. They really get their money's worth."

When she realized that clients with ongoing needs could benefit from their own systems, Corcoran established a consulting and training program, which helps a company quickly learn how to handle its own information requirements.

For Corcoran, Online has not only been a financial success; it has allowed her to remain a "generalist," a status she believes is the best of all possible worlds: "Online searching is an intellectual game," she says. "Sometimes it takes a very complicated strategy to find what you need, and sometimes it's just a matter of 'shaking up' the data base and seeing what filters out. The main thing is, you have to know how to learn quickly, and that's one of the great things that a generalist's approach allows you to do." As a quick learner, Corcoran is well on the way to becoming a Techno Age success story.

Project Theme II: Help people and businesses make or save money. Many successful Techno Age–style projects not only make money for the SE but also ultimately enable others to do the same. Newsletter publisher Charles Jasco, for example, has developed publications that save businesses money on items ranging from energy management devices to personal computers. Other

SE's, like Judith Garelick, have used their academic researching and teaching skills to learn the science of investing, and now make good livings counseling others on what to do to make their money grow.

"The li *of money is like the* li *of wisdom," proposed Master Hui. "It takes time and hard work to accumulate."*

"I think it is more like the li *of water," Shen Ti countered. "You must put it in a strong container, or it will quickly flow away."*

Fun and games, Techno Age-style. Jerice Bergstrom (Norwich, VT) vividly remembers a morning chat with a neighbor almost four years ago. Her neighbor was complaining that she had just laid out more than fifty dollars to buy her son a hand-held video game. "Outrageous!" she had cried. "My son mastered the game in less than two weeks, so now it's just collecting dust on a shelf. Too bad there isn't a toy pool where I could have cheaply picked up somebody else's dust collector," the neighbor sighed.

Jerice agreed with her neighbor; she even turned it into a project. Together with her husband, Jon, Jerice invented the Toybrary, which lends high-tech products and toys to individuals and institutions all over Vermont. At the Toybrary you can find anything from video games and software programs to fancy electronic typewriters and espresso machines. The Toybrary works on the same principle as a conventional book library: members pay a yearly fee for the privilege of borrowing "toys," and they agree to pay for any demolished or lost items, as well as cover the maintenance costs for things like computer printers, which need expensive ribbons.

Although the idea immediately intrigued the Bergstroms, it took several years to thoroughly research high-tech and toy industries for possible "acquisitions," followed by careful testing of various gadgets on their own children and friends. Today the Toybrary lists more than fifteen hundred items in its catalog.

"The idea of a library is nothing new," says Jon Bergstrom. "We just made it compatible with the new toys available these days. We're pleased that the Toybrary provides a service to the community that allows people to experience things for a fraction of the purchase cost. It fills an important need that we think will only continue to grow."

Project Theme III: Provide new ways for people to teach and learn. Every Soft-Skilled Entrepreneur has been a student, and many have been teachers in love with learning. Some of the smartest teachers have discovered that the Techno Age has created unprecedented opportunities for cashing in on their life's love outside the system. Former teacher Mary Rohon, for example, now makes a living teaching parents how their children can learn through toys. Another teacher turned SE, Bernard Tessler, made his mark selling educational software and games.

"Would you describe the li *of education as the transfer of ideas?" asked Master Hui.*
Shen Ti pondered this question before replying. "Yes, but it is also a process of mutual exchange. Therefore I would describe the li *of education as a thundercloud. It absorbs moisture from the river but replenishes the current with its rainfall."*

The case of the unintentional software business. Peter Dublin (Watertown, MA), president of Intentional Educations Inc., a company that develops educational materials ranging from textbooks and workbooks to software programs, considers himself to be, above all, an educator.

Dublin formed Intentional Educations in 1976 as a non-profit organization dedicated to developing alternative educational materials for the Techno Age. All his people held full-time jobs outside Intentional, working simply to satisfy their idealism, until a $2,500,000 contract helped Dublin turn his passion into a thriving business.

The next breakthrough came when a publisher asked Dublin to work on a simple word-processing package for junior-high-school students. Dublin agreed, because, as he puts it, "You can't say no to your publisher." So Dublin assembled an *ad hoc* group to complete "Bank Street Writer," which became a software sensation. The success of Bank Street Writer brought in contracts from other publishers who wanted various learning packages written, and Intentional Educations now has more than thirty programs to its name, ranging from spelling aids to adventure games with an educational twist.

As an offshoot, Dublin perceived a need for a publication that would inform educators about new software releases and offer software publishers a specialty medium for reaching the schools. The result was *Classroom Computer News*, which quickly grew to a controlled circulation of 55,000 and brought in revenues of more than $80,000 a month. At that point Dublin decided he was in the development business, not the publishing business, and sold the magazine.

Although Dublin is not sure of software's future in schools, he has found it an exciting way to pursue new avenues of education. "It's both fun and stimulating," he says, "and it allows me to be a lot more creative than print does. But you have to remember that it's just a medium—it will never replace textbooks. If it goes, though, we're still in business, because our business is education. But as long as it's considered a valid tool, we'll find better ways to adapt it to the art of teaching."

Project Theme IV: Help people become self-sufficient. In the early seventies, self-sufficiency became a hot topic. In the Techno Age it is a vital one, because in the wake of new technologies we've become highly dependent on a flood of consultants and specialists. Do-it-yourself SE's, however, never shirk responsibility for their own well-being, and they fan the desires of others to do the same. Paul and Sarah Edwards, for example, help people become self-sufficient by overcoming the problems of working at home. Bob Moran teaches people how to become self-sufficient through small businesses suited to their skills and abilities. *This book itself is an SE project designed to help people break the bonds of dependency that keep them from achieving their life-style and financial goals!*

"You are an able and confident student, Shen Ti," observed Master Hui. "One day you will know all that I know and we must part."

Shen Ti's eyes saddened, then brightened. "I now grasp the meaning of the ancient saying 'Independence is the greatest gift a teacher can bestow on his student.'"

Building a living from the ground up. Like many college grads of the sixties, Pat and Patsy Hennin (Bath, ME) trod the traditional path from school to marriage and graduate school. Patsy earned a master's degree in French literature at Tufts University, and soon found a job as a high school French teacher. With Patsy's help, Pat attended the University of Maine Law School and after graduating accepted a job with a law firm in Portland, Maine, which at this point seemed a perfect place to settle down and raise two sons. Unfortunately, when the practice of law did not satisfy Pat's spirit, he decided to abandon the profession.

Pat felt confident that his innate abilities would carry him toward something satisfying, but what? Having been raised on a farm in Canada, he had learned at an early age to value practicality and self-sufficiency. Throughout his youth he had built and repaired everything from airplane hangars to guesthouses and greenhouses. And while Patsy had been raised in a different setting, she too is a practical, self-reliant person. As she says, "I'd always baked our bread and made our clothes, so I was surprised when friends and neighbors asked us how to make clothes, how to fix cars, or how to install insulation. We considered these things to be basic parts of living."

The Hennins' spirits found liberation when Pat accepted an offer to build a house for an associate at his old law firm. He began by researching all the aspects of building a house, and then tapped every skill in his repertoire of experience. A year later he had built the first passive solar house in Maine, a feat widely praised by the national media. Following the publicity, the Hennins found themselves besieged with requests from people who wanted similar houses. "We took a look at each other," says Patsy, "and we decided that we could make a living building houses. I took some accounting classes at the University of Maine so I could manage the business end of things. Pat continued researching and learning more of the technical side."

At this point one would have expected that the Hennins would become contractors or start a small construction company. Instead, they ventured on a novel course: "We decided," says Patsy, "that we could either build houses, one after another, or teach people how to do it themselves. We liked the second idea, because even if they hired someone to do it for them, they would have a good idea of how a house was put together. Also, society seemed full of highly educated people who wanted access to practical skills, so they could do things for themselves. It seemed clear that we had some ability to work with people, and felt we could help them use their undeveloped capabilities."

That line of thinking led to the 1974 opening of the Shelter Institute, in Bath, Maine, the first school to teach people everything they need to know about building a house, from the foundation to the roof. At the Institute, students learn about basic planning, drafting, construction, wiring, plumbing, even solar energy. Lecture classes are held in the mornings, followed by hands-on practice sessions in the afternoons. In three weeks, students accumulate enough knowledge to build a house that is not only attractive and energy-efficient but also compatible with their physical and economic needs. Across the board, they save one-half the cost of building a conventional house. A three-week session costs $400 per person, $650 per couple.

After ten years, the Shelter Institute has become the most popular owner/builder school in the country. Its success rests as much on the Hennins' philosophy as it does on their technical expertise. "It can be the most elating three weeks in your entire life," says Pat. "A house is usually the largest personal investment anyone ever makes. And when you feel in control of that investment, you feel in control of your life."

Project Theme V: Stimulating Enjoyment and Recreation. SE's know that the Techno Age will naturally produce more leisure time for people. The more machines perform routine tasks and the more complex life becomes, the greater the need for creative and pleasurable diversions. That's why games like Trivial

Pursuit and unusual consumables like Richard Motta's Chipwiches have been so successful. Other SE projects, such as Thomas Barquinero's high-class campsites for nonoutdoor types, enable people to enjoy their leisure time in new and creative ways.

"We have been working hard," said the Master. "Do you wish you had more time to play?"

Shen Ti did a cartwheel. "Why, Master Hui, our work is our play. And our play, work. Have you forgotten the yin and yang of life?"

"No, Shen Ti. That is the joy of teaching. My students bring out the child in me." And with that the old man performed a cartwheel of his own.

Breaking the code of success. Six years ago Warren Holland (Norfolk, VA) got fed up with sitting in court while lawyers haggled over how much money delinquent clients owed his company. That decision marked the end of his career in the construction business and the beginning of a brilliant entrepreneurial adventure. It all began when Holland read an article in *Smithsonian* magazine about the exploits of Thomas Jefferson Beale, who allegedly buried a treasure in the Blue Ridge Mountains in the late 1800's, leaving behind a code that would-be treasure hunters would have to break before they could locate the loot. Although no one ever cracked the code, a lot of people had tried. Holland decided to go one step further and create his own treasure hunt.

After spending six months studying the science of cryptography, Holland invented Decipher, an elegantly packaged jigsaw puzzle with numbers printed on the top and bottom of each piece. Once players have assembled the challenging puzzle, they must crack a code based on a hidden correspondence between the printed numbers and the letters of the alphabet. The winners would not only get a lot of personal satisfaction from figuring out the code, but they would share a $100,000 reward if the code was cracked before a certain date. Holland provided one small clue to all players: the key to the code can be found in a novel by one of twenty-one authors mentioned in the instructions.

Says Holland, "I wanted to use my creativity, and I liked the idea of starting a national challenge. So I created a puzzle that I thought would be fun and would have a 'hands-on' feeling everyone could get involved in. The puzzle intrigues people, I think, because they find it exciting and stimulating. Besides, people always like to test their limits, and I think Decipher does it well." Apparently it did, because Holland sold more than 200,000 Decipher puzzles in less than one and a half years. Thirty-six people, ranging in age from 15 to 32 in 17 states solved the puzzle, within the stipulated time-frame, each one winning approximately $3200. The success has spawned a sequel, Decipher II, and a company that produces a growing line of games and puzzles, each with a unique twist to tantalize the player.

Project Theme VI: Make life easier for people at home and on the job. This theme attracts a great many Soft-Skilled Entrepreneurs. In fact many SE services and products revolve around easing the burdens of the Techno Age home and work environments. Some entrepreneurs, like Sharon Arkin, who created Therapist Preview (Chapter 1), and Alfred Poor, who researches the most cost-effective computer systems for schools, help people make better purchasing decisions. Other SE's, like RoJean Loucks (see below), offer a product or service that eliminates nuisance situations.

"Who knows the li *of comfort?" asked Master Hui.*
Shen Ti replied, "The li *of comfort is like the* li *of desire. Just when you should be satisfied, you grow restless again."*

How to nurse a healthy business. When RoJean Loucks (Asaria, KS) whipped up her first dress pattern, she didn't foresee that it would eventually lead to a full-time business. She had simply designed an outfit that could be worn while nursing, the sort of discreet, comfortable, and fashionable clothing she couldn't find in stores. Today Loucks and her sister, Jane Hull, design and produce clothing patterns for nursing mothers all over the country. Their company, "Babe too," has distributors throughout the U.S. and Canada, and is arranging for distribution in several foreign countries.

Louck's original idea evolved into a project when it dawned on her that the need for nursing clothing must be universal. An informal survey of other nursing mothers confirmed her thinking, but, to her surprise, the major pattern manufacturers whom she approached showed no interest in her idea. Fortunately, she didn't let their attitude hold her back from following her idea. In true SE style, Loucks and her sister began designing and marketing the patterns themselves. Their clothing designs use fabric overlays and other "invisible openings" allowing mother to discreetly nurse in public. The result is a line of patterns indistinguishable from contemporary fashions. As Loucks says, "Anybody who's nursed for any period of time longs, after a while, for something that doesn't button down the front or that isn't a shirt you have to pull out of a skirt. With our designs women can nurse discreetly and comfortably. That all adds up to a better and richer nursing experience. It's also the real story behind our success."

Project Theme VII: Serve as a Broker Between Two Parties in Need. A good project often comes about when an SE finds a way to connect two people who can benefit from each other. Alex Randall links people who have used computers to sell with people who want to buy micros at bargain prices. Rohn Engh's *Photoletter* connects photographers with photo editors and photo illustrators. And Freddie Kay brokers advertising to cable networks.

"*Who gains most from the* li *of commerce?*" *Master Hui asked.* "*The buyer or the seller?*"
"*Neither. It is the one who introduced them,*" *insisted Shen Ti,* "*because that person shares both their joys.*"

A *case of minding one's own business.* While working as a book-keeper in the evenings, Susan Hauser (New York, NY) spent her days organizing a not-for-profit food co-op in Manhattan. The co-op took off slowly, and Hauser found herself working for free. But the investment eventually paid off when the co-op grew into a respected and well-stocked market. Hauser left the project feeling confident with her newfound organizational skills, but not so confident about continuing as a bookkeeper. If she could set up a co-op for no pay, why couldn't she set up her own business for high pay?

The answer came at a party one night when she half-seriously asked an optometrist friend if he knew of any lucrative businesses she could start with inspiration and good organizational skills. As it turned out, the optometrist had been cultivating just such an idea for years: an outfit that links eye specialists with labor unions that want to provide eye care for their membership. That idea, coupled with Hauser's skills and ambitions, launched Comprehensive Professional Systems, which the entrepreneurs started on a shoestring.

Using the tacit skills she had picked up from organizing the co-op, Hauser easily manages the company, while her partners provide expertise and marketing skills. The idea has flown so well that a number of people have offered to buy into or buy out the business. So far, the partners have no interest in selling.

Looking back, Hauser says, "I felt that I was always worried about somebody else's business. Besides all the things I was doing for no pay, I was worrying about my boss's checkbook, his money, and his payroll. I decided that was ridiculous. Now I've got the skills to be independent of someone else's paycheck, and I find it really invigorating. I believe the future has a lot in store for me."

Project Theme VIII: Enhance people's mental, physical, and spiritual well-being. In a broad sense, one could say that *any* SE project enhances someone else's well-being. While that may be true, many solid SE projects directly capitalize on the Techno Age realization that the responsibility for well-being ultimately rests with the individual. Entrepreneurs like Stephanie Anderson, a fitness expert who helps people design custom exercise programs, provide the tools necessary for people to make positive

changes in their lives. Others, like Tom Chappell, manufacture
or distribute food or personal-care products free of dyes, chemicals, and other potential health hazards.

   "Do you agree that the li *of good health is the absence of
illness, Shen Ti?" asked Master Hui.*
   "No. The li *of good health lies in the mind's enjoyment of
the absence of illness."*

They exercised sound business planning. Two years ago, Bente
Strong (Dallas, TX) found herself waiting to change planes in an
airport, with nothing to do. She didn't want to guzzle watery
Scotch in the airport bar, and she didn't want to hang around the
newsstand browsing through magazines and papers. Besides, she
was on crutches, and felt hot and uncomfortable. What she really wanted was a nice cool shower—no easy feat in an airport,
where you either have to check into the Hilton or climb into the
drinking fountain. When Strong reached her destination, she described her unpleasant traveling experience to her friends Marianne Williams and Gayle Moeller, who empathized with
Strong's plight and jokingly suggested they open an oasis for
weary air travelers. But as so often happens, a half-serious suggestion can sow the seed of a flourishing SE project. Within days,
Moeller, Strong, and Williams were working on plans for Air
Vita: a comfort center in airports, where travelers between
flights can check their bags, work out, use a sauna, get a mas-
sage, and shower—all within an hour.
   "In the early days," Moeller says, "we said to ourselves, 'This
can't be such a brilliant idea—it's so logical. Why isn't anyone
else doing it?'" To find out, they called airport hotels and clubs
all over the country and asked if they provided athletic, napping,
or showering facilities for travelers. Each one said "No, but it
sounds like a good idea."
   Still unsure that their project would work, Strong moved to
New York, and Moeller moved to Los Angeles, where they sepa-

rately researched the idea further. Williams, unable to devote herself to the project full-time, decided to take on an indirect role in the research efforts. "We did all that research to overcompensate for the fact that we didn't have MBA's," Strong chuckles. "We had to really identify what we were doing. We had to think of every possible troubleshooting question someone might ask us."

Most important, Strong and Moeller turned up the fact that their idea perfectly tied into the growing national fitness trend. This was confirmed by John Naisbitt's *Megatrends*, which hit the bookstands while the two SE's were gathering information.

Confident of their findings, Moeller and Strong pulled together the necessary funding and convinced officials at the Dallas International Airport to allow them to open the first Air Vita center. Since the center now overflows with pleased travelers, the partners plan to expand nationally and internationally in coming years.

"Our whole idea is based on careful observation of social and life-style trends," Moeller claims. "As air travel and the desire for personal fitness increase, the need for a support business like Air Vita will continue to grow. It's not going to develop overnight, but we're prepared for the long haul because we know the trends are here to stay."

Step 2: Perceiving the World as an SE

Once you've focused your thinking on Universal Project Themes, you'll become more sensitive to your own internal chemistry. Then you can listen for signals that you've stumbled on a hot project idea. The Soft-Skilled Entrepreneur's mind works like a sound analyzer that filters out *clicks!* from *clacks*. A *click!* is a pleasant resounding in the mind that indicates a harmonious connection between an idea and the marketplace. Often the message contained within a *click!* needs some decoding, but once it becomes clear, a good SE project may be just around the corner.

To stimulate *clicks!*, SE's feast on all the cultural media they can find, scanning even the most obscure headlines for possible project leads. A typical SE print media diet might include the following: at least two major daily newspapers; general newsmagazines such as *Time* and *Newsweek*; several general business publications, including *Business Week*, *Inc.*, *Nation's Business*, *Forbes*, *Fortune*, and, of course, *The Wall Street Journal*; one or two magazines devoted to entrepreneurship, such as *Venture* or *Entrepreneur*, a specialty newsletter such as *John Naisbitt's Trend Letter* or *Science and Technology*; at least one general arts-and-letters review such as *Atlantic*, *Harper's*, or *The New Yorker*; one funky culture publication such as *The Whole Earth Review*; one or two general science magazines such as *Science News*, *Science 84*, *Discovery*, or *Technology High*; one or two regional business and general culture publications (e.g., *New England Business*, *California*, *New York*, etc.); and one or more trade publications or newsletters in a specialized field of interest.

How in the world, you may ask, can one read all that stuff and still have time to work on a project? By "crunching." In computerdom, crunching means taking a huge basket of raw data and running it through one or more formulas to reduce it to a digestible and meaningful form. In SE-dom, crunching means pulverizing a mountain of information into a digestible package that bulges with potential *clicks!*

Crunching includes the following techniques: 1) scanning headlines, subheads, and contents pages for signs of interesting articles; 2) reading the *first and last paragraph* of any article that catches your eye (if something intrigues you, read it whole, clip it, summarize it, and stuff it in a file for rapid retrieval); 3) establish which regular columns or columnists consistently give useful information. Check them at the beginning of your sweep, applying the first-and-last paragraph technique. In addition to a healthy main course of publications, SE's consume TV newsmagazine segments and documentaries for dessert; a balanced media diet often leads to the best workings of the mind.

Master Hui noted, "The li of history is like the course of the river, always flowing downhill to accumulate in the ocean of the past. Is that true, Shen Ti?"

"That is true," Shen Ti affirmed, "but the river can also wear away its course. Thus, the li of history lies in the surprises the future holds for us."

Carefully read the following maxims. They will help you develop and fine-tune your ability to detect *clicks!* as you scan various media sources and go about your day-to-day routines.

Click! Maxim 1: Listen for the subtle sound of a key sliding into the lock that bars the door to a future trend. The first rumblings of a coming craze are small, often unnoticeable to those who have not trained their minds' ears to hear the *clicks!* Look for the early signals, then be the first to unlock the door to new opportunities.

Walking a sure path. Jill Fallon (Boston, MA), frustrated with her six-year-old practice of the law, quit and went to find something that better suited her abilities. Fallon first began working with her husband, who runs a public-affairs consulting firm, but she kept her ears tuned for projects that could nurture her creativity and bank balance. One day her keen interest in Boston's history *clicked!* with a subtle observation.

"The idea came all at once," says Fallon. "But it had been building up for a long time." Boston Walkabouts, Fallon's new company, sells historical soundtrack tours through Boston, in English, French, Japanese, and German. Each Walkabout is a recorded cassette that includes narratives, sound effects, dramatizations, songs, and music. Tourists using the tape get treated to history and entertainment as they experience the city's many historical sites.

Fallon had long thought about making historical information available to tourists. "I took my junior year in college abroad," she says, "and was frustrated by the lack of accessible historical information in English. That concern really stuck with me." What also struck her was the upswing in the numbers of tourists tromping down Boston's historic Freedom Trail. For months Fallon carefully watched TV spots and read newspaper articles about the increase in tourism. And when Sony introduced its Walkman cassette players, she heard a resounding *click!*

Because of her observation of current trends, all Fallon had to do was put two and two together. As she says, "My idea for 'audio souvenirs' is really timely. Tourists are pouring into town, and personal cassette devices are as common as can be. It's a great match."

Not all *clicks!* emerge from studying the cultural media; sometimes they come from one's own perceptions of the world or from one's experience and daily routines. Often a *click!* resounds when an SE spots a need that others overlook. Such gaps offer marvelous opportunities for SE's to make a contribution to the world and earn a tidy sum at the same time. Sometimes the needs may be age-old and simple, but have languished for years. Other times the needs may result from technologies that develop so fast they leave most of the world standing in bewilderment. Whatever the case, pay attention whenever someone says, "Why the hell doesn't someone invent a thingamajig?" Such a thingamajig could fill the hole in your pocket. That's why Soft Skilled Entrepreneurs keep a watchful eye on even the smallest events taking place in their immediate environment.

Click! Maxim 2: Never fly on autopilot: you never know what you'll miss. The best project ideas often lurk in everyday tasks. Examine your daily routines for clues to new opportunities: sometimes a project idea lies right under your nose.

Decals stick through thin and thick. Rita Press (Baldwin, NY) detected a project idea on a kitchen shelf. "I was looking for a business for a long time and this just seemed to happen. I thought there was a real need for dishwasher-proof labels," says Rita, founder of Labeleze. Dissatisfied with unappealing spice-bottle and other kitchen labels that couldn't survive the dishwasher, Press declared that someone ought to design more attractive and durable ones. But how to go about it?

One day while painstakingly scraping her kid's collegiate decals from her car windows with a razor blade, she heard a *click!* If three years of sun and snow and rain hadn't harmed those stubborn decals, would a dishwasher faze them?

When she approached a conventional offset printer with her idea, he told her it couldn't be done. Undaunted, she sought out a decal printer, who ultimately produced her special transparent durable mylar decals. With sample labels in hand, Press easily convinced local shops and supermarkets to stock her product. Today Press's labels can be found in supermarkets and gourmet shops from Texas to Maine.

Running a business has changed Press's life: "I've never felt

better," she says. "There's something special about doing it on
your own, achieving something yourself. And I very much like
the personal touch I can give my product. After all, it came right
out of my own kitchen!"

The final maxim for uncovering *clicks!* is perhaps the most
important, for it synthesizes the first two. By combining awareness of newly emerging trends with a keen sense of what is happening in your immediate area, you will be in an ideal position to
conceive projects that work on a "macro" and "micro" level, well
suited to the world about you and your immediate resources.

Click! Maxim 3: Look for pieces in search of a puzzle. Very
often a hot project will emerge when seemingly unrelated elements are put together. Always be on the lookout for people and
events that may be combined in ways that enable them to augment each other and act synergistically.

A sorcerer's apprentice in the Techno Age. "My goal in life is to
become a wizard," says Alex Randall (Boston, MA). "The wizard
is one who looks for that little something that can be poked, and
'Poof!'—there's a huge transformation." And Randall has been
poking around in various entrepreneurial ventures for the past
decade. He took his first shot at entrepreneurship as an undergraduate at Princeton, where he studied psychology. A lover of
rock-and-roll, Randall asked himself what it was that all musi-
cians had and what they lacked. Many at his school had talent,
but few had a sophisticated P.A. system. *Click!* Randall went out
and bought one, which he agreed to let any band use in return
for one hour of free music. Randall used the numerous free hours
he racked up to sponsor various events such as free concerts and
music festivals. Upon receiving his B.A. he was also given an
award for having done the most to promote music at Princeton.
Although the venture did not actually make any money, he re-
gards it as a major achievement because it gave him an important
entrepreneurial orientation.

His next venture involved a T-shirt business. What was it
that fairs and outdoor concerts lacked? Instant T-shirt printing.
Click! Randall was in business again. Unlike his first enterprise,
the T-shirt business made money, enough to support his graduate

studies at Columbia, where he received the school's first Ph.D. in general systems theory.

Once out of graduate school, Randall again looked for a missing link, and found one in the burgeoning world of micro-computers. "At Columbia I studied under Margaret Mead," says Randall, "and one of the key things she taught me is to always think of the whole planet at once. So I sat back and looked at what was happening, and saw that eventually computers would affect the whole world one way or another." Randall then began looking for ways to find a missing computer link, and, with a by-now-familiar *click!* conceived the Boston Computer Exchange (BCE). As Randall puts it, "BCE puts together three elements in a way that everyone wins: people who want good equipment for less can get it at a fair price; people who want to sell their systems have an outlet; and I make a small percentage for linking the two."

BCE started as a bootstrap operation, with all capital flowing back into the business. In less than two years it grew to the point where it could afford to buy office space and have a regular staff of ten full-time employees. Randall is now developing a plan whereby any computer store can become part of the Boston Computer Exchange without having to buy an expensive license or franchise agreement. Again, a win-win situation.

What other puzzles will the wizard solve? Since starting BCE Randall has developed a consulting firm that specializes in computer networking and communications, and he plans to put together an entrepreneurial venture involving software for foreign countries. "Computer communications and software will have an enormous evolutionary shaping force on everyone on this planet," he speculates, "and I want to make sure that the outcome is by our own design, rather than something that just happens to us. That process can be an enormous positive sum gain for everyone—I guess that's the magic I'd really like to help create."

Step 3: Researching Your Idea

The best project idea can't earn you a dime if it fails to reach the action stage. But before you actually put muscle behind your idea by presenting it to a financial backer, suggesting that your boss fund it, or putting your life savings on the line, you should painstakingly research all the factors that will influence its success. As SE and software marketer Jeff Strauss insists, "Research is the only thing between you and disaster. It keeps you from spinning your wheels, wasting your time, losing your money, sapping your energy, and getting burned. If you can't thoroughly research a business, you should just keep on dreaming." Fortunately, it's never too late to become a good sleuth.

First of all, you should divide your research into three basic categories: the concept, the customers, and the competition. Conceptual research focuses on the worthiness and timing of your project. Research into customers helps you figure out whether people will buy your idea, and competitive research identifies other people who are already making money from your idea or one like it.

You can tackle the categories in any order as long as you eventually consider each one, but it usually makes sense to begin with conceptual research. After all, if the idea doesn't hold up under scrutiny, why waste your time looking for customers or stalking competitors?

Conceptual Research: Is your idea worth a dime? And will it be worth a dollar tomorrow? Two aspects of conceptual research must always be considered: 1) the value of your project in the marketplace; and 2) whether or not your project's time has come (or hasn't already passed). As for the first point, see if your idea incorporates one of the eight Universal Project Themes discussed earlier in this chapter. Will it:

1. Save anyone time at home or at work?
2. Save or make money for people or companies?
3. Improve the teaching or learning process?
4. Help people become self-sufficient?
5. Entertain people or improve their leisure time?
6. Make life easier for anyone at home or on the job?
7. Link parties with complementary interests?
8. Improve people's mental, physical, or spiritual well-being?

If your idea doesn't at least tangentially touch upon one of these themes, it will be difficult to market, and you should probably head back to the drawing board.

If you do have to drop an idea, don't despair—there are plenty more where that one came from. For as SE Jeff Strauss has discovered, "The moment you start to see the world in terms of entrepreneurial opportunities, a floodgate of ideas opens up. Most will dry up and die a natural death, but there's an infinite reservoir to draw from. Have faith that the creative juices will always flow."

Once you're convinced that your idea has the right stuff to flourish in the marketplace, you've got to figure out whether now is the right time to act. Is this really the beginning of a new trend? Or is it the moment before the peak and the start of a decline? Don't be afraid to ride the leading edge of a coming wave. But if you're at the peak, you may find yourself paddling in shallow waters once the surge has passed.

SE Charles Levin suggests looking at project timing in the same way NASA looks for the right time to launch a rocket: "Scientists in the space program think in terms of 'windows,' a time when the right meteorological and astronomical conditions exist. If the window is closed or foggy, the launch gets canceled. An entrepreneurial idea is the same way; if you launch at the wrong time, you're likely to find your time, energy, and money burning up in a quick reentry."

How do you check your window? Read and talk. Locate and read every article that relates to your subject. Find proof that the timing is right and that the trend you're relying on isn't a flash in the pan. Then talk to experts in the field and others who are doing a project similar in form and structure to your own.

Lovella Williams used this approach and found a clear window for launching her software teaching center. Williams had worked as a marketing rep for various computer companies, including Xerox, and found that she spent most of her time teaching customers how to use the software packages they bought from her. Since she enjoyed teaching more than selling, she wondered if it was possible to make a living at it. So she researched the possibilities by reading every article she could find on software training and by talking to numerous professional contacts about the feasibility of starting her own school. After five months of probing and weighing the decision to leave the security of her job, she decided that the idea was not only timely but would also have staying power for a good many years to come.

Williams's Software Learning Center, Inc. is small, but she foresees rapid and inevitable growth: "I'm providing a service that people can no longer do without. Software is becoming much more important than hardware nowadays. If you don't know how to use the software, you're sunk. And everyone, from individuals to corporate employers, will insist on good training. It's an idea whose time has definitely come."

Customer Research: Who's going to buy your widget? Your idea seems brilliant on paper. It fits a Universal Project Theme. And you've established an open window. Do you begin the count-down? Not until you determine your destination with customer research, which not only locates likely buyers of your service or product but also proves that they will pay for it.

Customer research begins with sizing up potential buyers or clients—who are they, how many are they, and how do you reach them? If you're starting a publication or developing a product you can sell through direct mail, consult a mailing-list catalog to get some sense of the "universe," the total number of conceivable buyers of your product. If your project involves manufacturing a new kind of widget, visit the library for statistics on the estimated number of people who might conceivably purchase it. If you're about to offer a service to businesses or professionals, use trade and professional directories to isolate the total population you can reach by phone or mail.

Whatever the results, be conservative about how many people will actually buy whatever you're selling. The mere fact that seven million people own personal computers doesn't necessarily mean six million of them will leap to buy your hand-knit dust covers. As a rule of thumb, don't bank on more than one-half to one percent of the target audience buying your goods. Simple multiplication of that range times your intended selling price will reveal your potential gross income.

The more you know about your audience, the more you minimize your risks. Rebecca Durfee, who joined several friends and relatives to form a retail store that sells educational software and trains families on PC's, recalls how she and her partners examined every conceivable angle. "We went over population statistics and projections to see what our area looks like now and will look like in the future. We even looked at what kind of new streets and what kind of shopping malls would be going in. We knew our market would be changing all the time and we wanted to be on top of it."

Once you've sized up your audience, how do you find out if they'll really pay cash for your product? Simple. Ask them. Laurel Gruenwald, co-founder of Interpersonal Software, says that she and her partner ". . . talked to all kinds of people who might be interested in taking our type of [software learning] classes. We chose people who work in related fields and who might benefit from our business. A lot of people thought it was a great idea."

What if your project involves a new widget rather than a service? Same approach. Ask friends and family if they'd actually buy one if they saw it in the store or in a catalog. Then take a prototype around to various distribution outlets to get some feedback from people who make a living selling goods like yours. (You might even be able to land a few orders in the process.)

You can test projects that involve services or publications by calling or surveying potential buyers to find out what they like and don't like about other products similar to yours. (This enables you to find out what you need to know without revealing any secrets.) However you do it, validate your thinking in the real world.

Alex Randall sums up this kind of research with the following principle: "Never commit to a final media before the sale is made." That means, don't sink all your money into a project until you're sure the sale can be made. Randall offers the following example. "When I started my T-shirt business, I knew that the risk was getting stuck with a huge and expensive inventory that I couldn't sell. I solved this problem by purchasing a portable imprinting machine that I could take to fairs and other gatherings and print the design at the time of the sale. This approach saved me from disaster in the early stages of the business, back in 1973. I had a new pattern that said 'Streak for Impeachment.' I figured that I could sell at least five hundred shirts at an upcoming rally; however, on the day of the event Nixon resigned and the T-shirts were moot. Had I printed them ahead of time, I'd have been stuck with unsalable goods. Instead I was stuck with a fifty-dollar pattern and five hundred shirts that could be used with any of the other four hundred patterns I offered. I think this lesson can be applied to just about any business."

Competitive Research: Is there anyone else out there? SE's know that in the free-enterprise laboratory, even the most novel project idea will eventually clone a competitor or two. That's just the nature of entrepreneurial DNA. SE's use the following approach to investigate competitive gene slicing: 1) locate every potential competitor; 2) examine their strengths and weaknesses; 3) get them or their customers/clients to teach you what they know about the field.

Newsletter publisher and information specialist Richard Golob used this approach when doing the competitive research for a new publication. "Once you've found out who your competitors are, you have to get hold of their publications and see what they're doing," he says. "Then see how you can differentiate yourself, as well as incorporate some of their good features. In that way your publication has what theirs has, and more. In addition, it's a good idea to informally poll the people you think are your prime target group and ask them what publications they now receive, and what they do and don't like about them. This is also useful in shaping your own publication and improving in areas where your competition is weak."

Like their military counterparts, SE's do reconnaissance missions on their competition. Pretend you're a potential customer with ready cash, and your competitors will tell you everything they know. Rebecca Durfee's group did something like that before starting its enterprise: "To check out the competition, we looked at ads from outfits that might be doing the same thing. We visited stores and acted as shoppers, learning all we could. As it turned out, there was no one doing the exact same thing as we planned to do, and that made us feel good."

What happens if you do discover competitors? Abandon your project? Head back to the drawing board? Not necessarily. SE's know that competition isn't always bad; in fact, if you can provide better services or goods for less money, you can actually turn existing competition to your advantage. Healthy competition also keeps you on your toes, forcing you to think of new and creative strategies. What counts is the size of the market and what share your competitors control. Norman Shum, founder of China Belle, a Chinese fast-food chain, sums up his point of view this way: "If you go into your own business, you will be in the same water as the giant corporations. It's like a pie. If you have the stronger, bigger knife, you can cut a bigger share. But if you can't have a bigger knife, then create a new pie and make it the very best."

Step 4: Putting It Down on Paper: Developing an SE Flight Plan

Let's assume you've developed a brilliant project idea, have found an eager audience, see a clear window, and have something your competitors don't. Push the launch button, right? Not quite. Before blasting beyond the pull of gravity, you need a written flight plan detailing your course and your destination.

Such a document might seem superfluous at this point, but it can help you by: 1) quickly showing you any overlooked details; 2) helping secure financial or other support; 3) giving you a specific schedule; and 4) reminding you of your important financial and life-style goals. Whether the project succeeds or fails, at a later date the flight plan can tell you where you miscalculated and guide you to a more successful launch in the future.

The SE Flight Plan contains the following sections: 1) a general description, which summarizes the essence of the idea; 2) a rationale for the project; 3) a listing of the competition; 4) possible funding sources; 5) a marketing plan; and 6) future enhancements, with budget and revenue projections.

At this stage you can begin working on sections one through three. As you read through the next three chapters you'll be able to fill in sections four through six. But don't wait until the end of the book to begin your Flight Plan. That way, when you finish this book, you won't have to wait for an instant to start practicing all you've heard preached in its pages.

PROTECTING YOUR IDEA

Once you've written an SE Flight Plan you might feel slightly paranoid about showing it to people, for fear someone might rip it off. To make money with an idea, though, you'll eventually have to tell someone about it. So what can you do to protect it?

Although you can seldom fully protect an idea, you can draw up a confidentiality or "nondisclosure" agreement that swears the other party to secrecy. Bear in mind that like most agreements, however, they only work with honest people. Since anyone who really wants to steal your work can do so, always know who you're dealing with before you disclose any information that might be valuable.

Once you're ready to reveal what you're doing, you can employ three mechanisms of protection offered by the government. One is copyright, which applies to written materials and other works involving artistic expression, including computer programs (note that it covers the *expression* only, and not the ideas). As the name suggests, copyright prevents other people from taking materials you've written and using them in whole or in part without your permission (which you may want to grant for a fee or publicity). Although copyright protection takes effect the instant ink begins flowing from your pen, when you release copies of your work to the outside world, cover it with the word "Copyright," followed by a capital C enclosed in a circle, the year, and your name. This ensures your later rights if someone does try to rip off your work. Without the copyright notice you have no right to sue anyone else. (Not that having the notice guarantees you a victory in court—you still have to prove that the offending party used actual material from your work.) To be safe, put a copyright notice on everything you present to the public, including advertising. For maximum protection, you can officially apply to register your claim to copyright on forms supplied by the Copyright Office (see SE Library, Section I).

Trademark offers another form of protection, covering brand names for products and services. Whenever you see a little TM beside a name or slogan, it means that someone claims ownership of the trademark. This may sound circular, but a person acquires rights to a trademark by using it. Selecting, using, and applying for federal registration of a trademark is tricky and requires extensive searching from a *qualified* trademark firm and an attorney who specializes in such matters. The costs can range from $200 to $1,000.

The third type of protection is a patent, which prohibits other people from making, using, or selling products that embody your invention. Like trademarks, patents require technical expertise. Once you've got a prototype of your invention or feel confident that you have a viable idea, hire a patent attorney to begin evaluating the novelty of your brainstorm before going to the time and expense of securing protection.

It's especially important to see a patent attorney if you have any inclinations to take your widget to invention-marketing services. While some of these services are legitimate, others are not. Those in the latter category don't make their money through royalties on your widget, but by tapping your own wallet. You can pay hundreds, even thousands of dollars for useless or boilerplate reports and reams of public-domain census data masquerading as "marketing research." You can also wind up losing your rights to patent your invention. So check with your patent attorney before hooking up with any invention-marketing service that claims it will put you on the road to fame and fortune. (See the SE Library, page 196, Legal, for an informative guide to protecting your ideas.)

To sum up, never be paralyzed for fear of someone stealing your idea. If others can do a better job with your idea faster, you can't do much to stop them. The best way to protect yourself is to act fast and smart. And leave all potential copycats in your dust.

EXERCISE 4: LISTENING FOR CLICKS!

Read over the following ideas that were taken from several common publications. Try to think of them in terms of Universal Project Themes and other topics discussed in this chapter. What *clicks!* go off in your mind as you read them? Try coming up with at least two or three project ideas for every *click!* you get. Then head out to the library and try finding other cultural media sources that stimulate your thinking.

1. *Forbes* magazine reported that the sales of home gym equipment are booming. Consumers are buying everything from personal heart monitors to scaled-down Nautilus machines and treadmills. A *New York Times* article reports that private companies are spending a · record amount to keep their workers fit.

2. The *New York Times* noted that tourism is on an all-time rise. One related phenomenon is the increasing number of colleges and vocational schools offering training in the travel field.

3. According to *The Wall Street Journal*, colleges cannot keep up with the demand for computer courses. A *Boston Globe* article documented the problem at MIT and also noted that it is a nationwide problem.

4. *U.S. News & World Report* described how an increasing number of companies are starting programs through which employees can work at home via computers. The main problem that managers have with the programs, though, is that they cannot adequately evaluate the work done by "Telecommuters."

5. *Money* magazine noted that the demand for second-hand computer equipment is on the rise and that several outfits and publications are devoting shelf space and ad space to the used-computer market.

6. A *New York Times* article describes how several cottage industries have evolved around SAT preparation, including private schools, workbooks, and computer programs.

7. An article in *The Wall Street Journal* describes the exploits of a writer who is reaping the benefits of working in public—that is, in store windows. She sets up her typewriter and writes short stories while people outside pass her notes and read what she has written as she posts it on the glass. She finds inspiration in the crowds; the stores find customers.

8. *Esquire* magazine noted that workers in fast-paced positions, especially in high-tech industries, increased their productivity substantially when allowed to take a sabbatical. Similar programs that took these burnout-risk employees away from the daily grind of the office were also thought to be successful at increasing future creativity.

9. An article appearing in *Forbes* magazine described how an increasing number of physicians are being sued for malpractice because they aren't aware of the latest medical technology available to them. The article suggests a strong need for new ways of keeping doctors abreast of breakthrough technologies in their own and related fields.

10. *The New York Times* ran an article stating that many young executives eat "on the go," with rarely enough time to sit at a lunch counter, much less cook a meal.

5
STARTING ON A SHOESTRING: BASIC SE BUSINESS TACTICS

The early-spring thaw enticed Master Hui and his disciples out-
doors, where the Master could turn everyone's attention toward
developing physical prowess through "the ways of the crane and
the tiger." Crouching in the low, powerful stance of the jungle
cat, Master Hui posed a question. "If a tiger challenged you, how
would you respond?"

Shen Ti bowed respectfully and assumed the stance of the
crane. "I would choose the way of the crane, for quick escape."

Master Hui then lunged, and with a flashing sweep of his
foot knocked Shen Ti to the ground. "And when the cat strikes
before you can take wing?" Master Hui asked as he helped Shen
Ti to his feet.

Rubbing a sore elbow, Shen Ti answered, "I would move
with greater wariness, maintaining perfect balance. By doing so
I could always take flight before the tiger struck."

"Why not counter power with power?" asked the Master,
springing toward Shen Ti and aiming a flying side kick at the
young man's chest. Shen Ti twisted away, ducked the blow, and
used Master Hui's own momentum to easily trip him to the
ground. It was the Master's turn to rub a sore elbow. "Very good.
You understand the power of quickness, Shen Ti. Strength alone
can be a false ally."

GOING BEYOND THE DREAM STATE

SE project ideas may provide grist for the dream mill, but they won't put peanut butter on your table or socks on your feet unless you can translate them into reality. This chapter will issue you a passport from the dream world to the nuts-and-bolts business world. To make that great leap forward, you need a good broom to sweep your path free of basic start-up issues such as digging up seed money, selecting and setting up the right kind of business structure, and deciding whether to bring in partners. In short, regardless of your unconventional style, you must become a bona fide business person.

INVEST BRAINS, NOT BUCKS

Nothing depresses small business people more than finding themselves midway into a hot project without enough money to keep the business alive. In fact, according to just about every traditional textbook on small business, "undercapitalization" kills more new ventures than any other disease. Soft-Skilled Entrepreneurs, however, immunize themselves by defining lack of funds as a blessing. How can being broke be a blessing? It forces you to substitute creativity for dollars. Some of the most poorly capitalized SE's have turned shoestrings into fortunes. Instead of renting high-rise space, they started off in their garages until the businesses got rolling; instead of buying new equipment, they bartered for it or begged it from an overstocked dealer glad to get rid of it for small monthly payments; instead of buying a fleet of delivery trucks, they found someone whose fleet was only partially used and welcomed some extra income; in short, instead of spending their time and energy looking for funding, they looked for ways to "shoestring" their businesses into existence.

"Shoestringing" has been made popular by Arnold Goldstein, a bankruptcy attorney who has rescued hundreds of small businesses from extinction, started at least twenty enterprises with no money down, and has even written several excellent books on the subject (see SE Library, Section I). Says Goldstein, "Most of the time when I'm called in to help bail someone out, I find them sitting behind an aircraft-carrier-size mahogany desk in a plush office. While the fixtures look great, the balance sheet stinks, and they're going down the tubes in style. They'd have been much better off if they'd invested in a bridge chair and made a desk out of two orange crates and an old door. Think lean, only spend your money on things that will *make* you money. That's the number-one and most frequently violated rule of the shoestring entrepreneur."

ROUNDING UP OPEC

If starting on a shoestring is the first rule, the second is: put in as little of your own money as possible. Some kinds of businesses, though, can't get by totally with bartering or other shoestring techniques, and require a dose of cash to get off the ground. What do you do if you don't want to risk the money in your savings account? Easy. You go fishing for "OPEC": Other People's Excess Cash. OPEC is usually the best way to fund a project, because even if you fail, you'll still have your house, car, pedigree Abyssinian cat, and anything else you've worked hard to own. And even if you do have to pay back your lender and creditors, you can usually do so at a pace that enables you to dust yourself off and try again.

OPEC comes in many forms: loans from family members or friends; credit from customers, clients, and suppliers; bank loans; cash injections from venture capitalists. Each form offers advantages and disadvantages that should be carefully weighed before casting your lure. The following sections provide tips on selecting a funding source or mix of sources best suited to your own needs and situation.

TAPPING FRIENDS AND RELATIVES

The search for OPEC usually begins close to home; in fact, right at your own kitchen table. Sanford Schwartzman, who has used every conceivable form of OPEC at one time or another, likes "kitchen-table money" the best. Kitchen-table money comes when you sell your idea to the people who know and trust you the most. Your SE Flight Plan will come in handy here because it answers everyone's questions in a businesslike way.

If your friends and family believe in you, they'll probably be easy to convince; however, their money does not come without some attached strings. Your best friend or sister-in-law may be warmer to your idea than a coldhearted banker, but if you fail, you may find your personal relationships with such people severely strained. You must therefore ask the following important questions before inviting others into your investment group.

First, can they *afford* to lose the money? Those who invest (and this goes for yourself) must be playing with "match" money, money they can afford to hold over a lit match and kiss good-bye. Watch for facial expressions and other body language when you tell friends and relatives that they might lose their dough. Better yet, you probably know them well enough to ask them how the loss would affect their lives. Encourage them to be honest. Ask yourself how *you'd* feel if the situation were reversed, and they did it to you.

Second, even though people may be able to afford the loss, how would they feel about *your* losing it? Would they lose respect for you, never be able to trust you again, or find their fondness for you diminished? If so, don't take their money. As Charles Levin warns, "No amount of money can ever be worth the risk of damaging a good relationship. I'd let all my ideas go straight to hell before losing a single friend."

"Tell us about safety in numbers, Shen Ti," urged Master Hui.

Shen Ti did not hesitate. "When I walk with my companions, their strength is my strength."

"But what if your companions do not share your courage?"

"Then their weakness is my weakness."

The sweet taste of success. Three years ago, psychiatrist Victor Syrmis (New York, NY) pounded the New York City pavement in search of the perfect birthday gift for his wife. After hours of frustration, Syrmis wandered into a store that specialized in casting marble, bronze, or gold busts from black-and-white photographs. The idea intrigued Syrmis, but he wasn't sure he could live with a permanent bust of himself on the mantel. So he asked the proprietor if he could fashion a bust out of something less permanent, like chocolate. The proprietor just laughed Syrmis out of the shop.

Deciding he wanted the last guffaw, Syrmis studied etching and drawing, toyed with foils and adhesives, and then refined techniques of melting and molding chocolate. His experimentation ultimately led to a reliable method of making chocolate relief sculptures from photographs. It also led to a business, Chocolate Photos.

In order to raise money for his enterprise, Syrmis threw two gala parties: "I rented a club, invited all my friends and anyone else I could think of. There were chocolates, negatives, and photographs everywhere. The whole thing was very elegantly done. I passed my business plan around and got those who showed any interest to write down their names. Later on, I called them all and sent them follow-up letters asking if they were willing to invest. I sold thirty-five shares at four thousand dollars apiece. One hundred and forty thousand dollars was just enough to get the company going."

So Syrmis partitioned his office, seeing his psychiatry patients on one side and selling Chocolate Photos on the other. When one patient complained of dreaming about chocolates, he was eventually forced to move his practice next door. Syrmis's investors certainly aren't complaining, though; in less than a year Chocolate Photos sold 75,000 reproductions at $35 apiece. And with new automation in the works, Syrmis predicts even better sales next year.

LET YOUR CUSTOMERS, CLIENTS, OR SUPPLIERS FOOT THE BILL

A wily SE goes beyond friends and relatives to another ready source of OPEC: those who buy your wares and those who sell you the materials you need. Many small businesses have been started (and maintained) on deposits for merchandise or advance payments for services yet to be rendered. But be sure you can come through with the goods once you've got other people's money in hand; otherwise you might find yourself stuck with "pay-up-front" terms for many years to come.

One SE, who prefers to remain anonymous because of the confidential nature of his work, used the customer-financing approach to start a data-shredding service. Several years ago this astute SE realized that the microcomputer boom in business would bring with it a proliferation of sensitive data and information that people wouldn't want hauled to an ordinary dump. To exploit this growing Techno Age problem he came up with a shredding and disposal service that would serve financial institutions in his city, but he needed some capital to get started. An SE in spirit, he turned adversity into advantage by visiting a junkyard to find equipment that would sufficiently shred or mangle computer printouts beyond recognition. The total outlay was fifteen dollars. Next, he personally marketed the service to several large banks, and walked away with a two-month trial contract that gave him a nice advance payment. With the cash in hand, he hired a truck and a couple of helpers to pick up the bank's printouts, which he shredded in his garage and then sold to a recycler. Within a year, this SE gained command over the data-shredding market in his entire metropolitan area. Yes, starting off broke can be a blessing. If he'd borrowed the money to rent space, bought shiny new equipment, and hired a staff, he would have achieved no better results than he did with his fifteen-dollar investment. The difference, of course, is spelled p-r-o-f-i-t.

As with clients and customers, suppliers can also float your enterprise until your cash flows positively. If your business plan looks solid and you present it confidently, you can often convince a supplier to give you favorable credit terms, perhaps a ninety-day payoff, especially if you offer to pay a top price. Better yet, suggest that you'll buy exclusively from him or her once the business takes off. It's a win-win situation; as you grow, so will your inventory needs. The downside? If you fall behind, your supplier will have to hound you for the money. So before you make such arrangements, be sure that your sales will eventually enable you to pay your bills.

"The wise warrior avoids battle whenever possible," noted Master Hui. *"Tell us the best way to do this, Shen Ti."*

"The wise warrior engages his opponent in counsel," Shen Ti replied, *"convincing him that more will be won by joining forces than by carrying out warfare."*

A *cable success story.* Freddie Kay (Stamford, CT) dropped out of Colorado College after two years because the academic life was just not for him. From there he went straight into sports P.R., which he also grew to despise as well. "I may have been the worst P.R. man in the country," he says. "I held ten jobs in five years." At that point Kay, deciding to give up P.R. altogether, landed a job in sales at a Boston radio station. "They looked at me," he says with a laugh, "and decided that I was sufficiently aggressive, hungry, and pushy."

Kay stayed in television and radio sales for seven years, working for CBS, and finally for ABC, until he felt he was overpaid, underworked, and poorly managed. So he decided to step back and take stock of his situation. "I was tired of the corporate runaround," he says, "and I thought I had gained enough experience at CBS and ABC to start on my own. At that time cable television was booming, and I thought I'd try selling advertising, which I was good at, to the local cable networks."

Kay quit his job, then spent a year researching the industry and writing a business plan for Cable Ads USA, which he presented to various investors. Alas, none were willing to spend the money. Not about to let their negative response torpedo his idea, Kay decided to fund his plan guerrilla-style. Unable to afford office space, he bartered with a local production company: if they would provide him a small space, he would give them free advertising. Unfortunately, the production company went belly-up, leaving Kay shivering in the cold.

Kay picked himself up and again bartered for space, this time with a more solid landlord. Now he needed film equipment to produce his cable ads. Still without funding, Kay called on his more than ten years of sales experience to make friends with the equipment vendor, whose price he was able to talk down to acceptable terms. "Making friends with your vendors is about the smartest thing you can do," he says. "If they think you're doing a good business, they'll take a chance on you and give you a deal, because the bigger you get, the more equipment you'll need."

Kay eloquently summarizes the SE attitude: "No one should decide against a business for lack of funds. In reality, money is the last thing you need. More important, you need to commit, you need to be resourceful, you need good people around you, and you need to be able to listen to your people." That wisdom has enabled Kay to gross $350,000 in his first year, with strong prospects for major expansion in the years to come. Not bad for a business started with "no money down."

BORROWING MONEY FROM A BANK

Although most people who need OPEC first approach the local bank, doing so poses definite problems to the SE. Stuffy banker types often resist the schemes of zany entrepreneurs, and they always avoid risking loans to people who can't trot out lengthy track records, a wealthy co-signer, or strong collateral, such as a house that the bank can seize if an enterprise fails. While no law can stop you from using a personal loan to capitalize your project, you won't be able to borrow more than your assets, and you'll be putting them at risk.

Despite these problems and the often high interest rates on commercial money, there are some advantages to a bank loan. Once you repay the bank, you have no further obligation, no stock to share, and no partners to placate. (You can sometimes get a better deal on government money through the Small Business Administration and other agencies. See SE Library, Section VII.)

Some SE's put together the equivalent of a bank loan by taking maximum cash advances against credit cards. While it's fairly difficult for someone with no collateral to walk into a bank and get a loan for $20,000, almost anyone can walk into five banks and get five credit cards with four-thousand-dollar credit lines each. Bob Kuzara did just that to make his enterprise happen. Recalls Kuzara, "I was riding the subway to my new job as a CPA and was reading the business classified section of the newspaper. A custom-furniture-painting business up for sale caught my eye and really intrigued me. I thought about my new job behind a desk, looked at the ad again, and said to myself, 'What the hell, it's only two subway stops past where I'm supposed to get off.' I visited the business and called my wife, and she thought it was a great idea for us."

Instead of reporting to work, Kuzara reported to the bank for a $40,000 loan, which was promptly turned down. Several days later he met an officer of the bank on the golf course, and after talking with him for a while, got him to agree to an easier arrangement: the bank would put up $25,000 if Kuzara could come up with $15,000. On the day he had to close the deal for his new store, Kuzara wrote a check for $15,000, went around to the banks that issued his credit cards, took cash advances, then deposited the money in his checking account. That night he slept well. "It worked like a charm," Kuzara laughs. "As far as the bank was concerned, the transaction was as normal as could be. No one knew how it really came about."

Many other SE's have perfected "plastic financing" to a fine art. One master of the plastic is Dal La Magna, the legendary "Tweezerman." In five years La Magna attempted more entrepreneurial ventures than most SE's try in a lifetime, including a stab at water beds, an attempt to convert drive-in movie theaters to drive-in discos, a computerized dating service, and specially designed lasagna baking pans. All of these bombed for one reason or another. He finally struck gold with Tweezerman, which wholesales top-of-the-line tweezers to salons, drugstores, and department stores.

To fund the business, La Magna scrounged up $500 in cash and used two credit cards to finance the inventory he needed. To the surprise of skeptics who didn't believe there would be much demand for tweezers with a price tag of $15, in its first year La Magna's new venture grossed nearly $80,000. His second year, sales soared to $200,000, and by his fifth year reached $1,000,000. Tweezerman now has ten full-time employees and a manufacturing plant in Italy. La Magna has since acquired ten credit cards and uses cash advances against them to buy inventory when he finds himself short on cash. "I have an immaculate credit record," he boasts. "I've never bounced a check, never missed a payment. When I need a short-term loan, I never have to look beyond my wallet."

A strong word of caution: while plastic financing is easy, it does have drawbacks. The interest is sky high, and you do have to pay it back in monthly chunks. If you miss a payment or two, your credit record can remain marred for a long time. The best policy is to use plastic money as a last resort or for small supplemental loans during difficult times. Whatever the case, make sure you can pay back the debt on time.

If you ever do approach a bank for a conventional loan, the following suggestions will improve your chances of coming home with a check in hand:

1. *Polish your credit status*. Before looking at anything else, the bank will scrutinize your personal credit. If you've never borrowed money before, immediately start borrowing small sums, paying them back well before the due dates on the notes. Then continually increase the amounts until you can get what you need for your project. Many SE's make it a habit to borrow money regularly from their banks, even if they don't have an immediate need for cash. As one SE puts it, "The more money you borrow, the more the bank is going to trust you. Sure, you pay interest, but if you put the cash in a money-market account, you don't pay much. You're just buying borrowing power for when you really need it."

Since bankers also scan credit-card-payment history, you'll want to knock down any high credit-card balances, especially if you've been using "plastic financing." Bear in mind that you never want to signal that you're inching up to your credit ceiling.

2. *Develop a good relationship with your banker*. Each time you borrow money, make sure you deal with the same bank officer. Despite their pin striped suits and stuffy ways, bankers are people too, and they often make decisions based on "people" instinct as well as computer printout. Sell your banker on your idea. Offer a sample of your wares. Treat the banker like a partner in crime. If you've set up an office, invite the bank officer over for a quick tour, even if it's still a small operation. Seeing is believing, and getting the bank to believe in you will put capital in your pocket.

According to John Lesanto, assistant vice-president of Cambridge Trust (a bank that sees many entrepreneurial requests for money), "Having a good sense of the person can be a very important factor in deciding about a loan request. If the numbers are borderline, I often go with my gut feeling about whether the person can pull through on the repayment. That's why I like to see tangible proof that someone is working a real business, not just dreaming."

3. *Just the facts, ma'am.* Most bankers read documents backwards, starting at the bottom line before deciding whether or not to scan toward the top. Since bankers want to determine quickly if and when you'll be able to pay off the debt, attach realistic cash-flow projections to your loan application. Include your SE Flight Plan. The more supporting evidence you display, the better your chance of convincing your banker to part with some cash.

Finally, don't just drop off your loan application or submit it through the mail; spend five or ten minutes with your bank officer summarizing your case. Charts and graphs (which most bankers love) can enhance your presentation. However you create it, focus on projecting a reliable, dependable, hardworking impression.

When his disciples begged Master Hui to tell them a story of heroism, he obliged them with the brave feats of General Lao Hsing. "The great general never attacked if his opponent outnumbered him badly," Master Hui began, "but under orders to rouse the corrupt army of Fu, Lao Hsing encamped his army behind a hill not far away from the city gates. Knowing his enemy numbered 5,000, and his troops were only 2,000 strong, Lao Hsing ordered brought to his camp the colors and equipment of 2,000 swordsmen, 2,000 archers, 2,000 foot soldiers, 2,000 heavy chariots, and 2,000 light chariots. By night his men lit 10,000 fires and by day his 2,000 men took turns performing maneuvers first as swordsmen, then as archers, foot soldiers, and chariot drivers in turn. The enemy, frightened by this display of superior force, surrendered and threw open its gates. The spoils doubled Lao Hsing's victory."

Projecting the right image at the bank. Back in 1980, Jeff Mulligan (Wellesley, MA) and a friend worked as DJ's at a Babson College party. The party was such a rollicking success that the two students formed Crustations, a rock DJ service for campus parties. When his friend graduated, Mulligan, a junior at the time, found himself solely in charge of the business.

Three years later, when rock videos burst onto the scene and the youth of America shifted its loyalty from *M*A*S*H* to MTV, Mulligan decided to capitalize on this Techno Age opportunity. With borrowed equipment and tapes, he recorded a trial show that he introduced at one of his famous campus parties. Again, a rip-roaring success.

Once he decided to transform his service from record spinning to video projection, Mulligan came to a dreadful realization. He needed to buy equipment and rent videos. When he sat down to figure out the cost, he found that he needed $15,000. "When I first thought about getting into videos, I was very excited. But when I figured out how much money I'd need, I realized that I didn't have fifteen thousand dollars in the bank. I had more like fifteen."

Undaunted by the figures, Mulligan checked out some business books from the library and with guidance from one of his professors wrote a business proposal for Videostar, a video DJ party service.

Still unsure about obtaining his $15,000, Mulligan went to a prominent local businessman with his plan, hoping to make him an investor. "He liked the idea," says Mulligan, "but he wanted equity, and I wanted a loan. It didn't work out because we didn't have the same goals."

Finally Mulligan decided to give his local bank a shot. He had a personal savings account and a good credit rating, even though he had never accumulated a large sum of money. He put on a tie, and with his business plan under his arm, explained his idea to the banker. To his amazement, the bank approved a

$15,000 loan. Why did Mr. Pinstripe go for it? Suggests Mulligan, "The banker saw that I had a solid idea and a good plan to back it up. I think he also liked my initiative and creativity, and saw it as an investment in the youth of America."

Jeff Mulligan is now working toward his MBA and is still running Videostar on the weekends. With gross sales of $40,000 his first year, he may well have created the most lucrative work-study program in history.

DO SE'S AND VENTURE CAPITALISTS MIX?

These days we hear a lot about venture capital, mainly in the hard-driving fast lane of the Techno Age. But if you intend to catch some of this exotic seed money, abandon all illusions about snaring any with only a business plan. Venture capital is the hardest of all investment money to garner. First of all, venture capitalists take highly selective risks. Since only a small percentage of their projects will eventually produce a return on the investment, they'll fund only those ideas that can (quickly) reap huge rewards, thus paying for the failures as well.

In general, venture-capital firms disdain endeavors that require less than a $500,000 initial investment because the return probably wouldn't justify getting involved. When they do pitch in the cash, they watch their investment closely, sometimes saddling the entrepreneur with less-than-friendly and not-so-silent partners. Many start-ups actually reject venture capital because they don't want to cramp their style or find themselves pushed into meeting profit projections that might compromise their long-term goals.

Sanford Schwartzman sums it up this way: "Venture capital is a tough game today. It's not like the old days when people put up money in the spirit of seeing whether man could really fly, go to the moon, make lasers, or put ten thousand phone calls through a nearly invisible microchip. Today's venture capitalists are interested in one thing and one thing only: getting a large multiple of their investment back as soon as possible. Consequently, they're not interested in any 'me too' ideas, and they usually won't touch anyone who doesn't have a track record. If you think you've got what it takes, then the venture-capital route may be a good one for you. Just be realistic about the brilliance of your idea and the soundness of your capabilities."

Obviously, venture capital is probably the last stop on an SE's search for money. But whether you go for venture capital or any other source of OPEC, think of it as a game. This is the most important lesson about financing you'll ever learn: money clings to confidence, while anxiety and fear chase it away.

PICKING A WINNING TEAM

Once you've gotten your funding together, you'll want to figure out whether you want any partners. Sometimes your funding automatically ties you to a partner, such as a spouse or a venture capitalist. Whatever the case, you always want to be extremely cautious about those with whom you share your dream. Whereas you can usually solve or patch over money problems, people problems will make or break you. Here are some basic tips about partners:

1. *Deciding whether you want to work by yourself or with a partner entails a beneficial compromise.* While working alone gives you complete control, it's also a little scarier and lonelier, since you have to make all key decisions yourself. On the other hand, if your partner doesn't perfectly complement your personality and talents, he or she can make your life miserable. As Marilyn Dashe says, "Being involved in a partnership is just as intense as being involved in a marriage. You have to give and take, talk with each other, and grow with each other. And if things fall apart, the 'divorce' proceedings can be mighty ugly."

How do you make a beneficial compromise? Try a nonvoting board of directors made up of people who have expertise in various aspects of business but can't control you. You can often find board members who will serve without compensation, primarily for the prestige. Sponsor a dinner every two months, inviting your advisers to help you with any current problems. This technique also works with partnerships. Neil Duane's group, Boston Documentation Design, uses a board of directors to stopgap each aspect of the business for which Duane and his partners have no expertise. Duane comments that this approach has saved him from many costly mistakes.

2. *Avoid silent partners.* The history of business is replete with horror stories of silent partners who become unpleasantly vocal. Arnold Goldstein strongly advises against such arrangements, noting that "there are no such things as silent partners. I can think of dozens of cases where silent partners crept out of the woodwork and made things horrible for the unsilent ones. In one case the silent partner, who had control over the company, refused to let the other partners branch into a new and potentially lucrative area because he was satisfied with the way things were and didn't want to take any risks. As it turned out, the company missed an exciting opportunity for logical expansion. The anger reached the boiling point and the whole company eventually fell apart because of it."

3. *If you decide to work with a spouse, be prepared for the strain on your marriage.* About ten percent of the SE's cited in this book work with their spouses. Most recommend it to others but cite particular cautions about working with a person you live with and know so well. Freddie Kay, whose wife is a full partner in his business, suggests, "The most important thing is to listen. Listen, listen, listen, even when it hurts. For a while things weren't going well, and it was because we were stumbling all over each other's egos. We learned that we had to be flexible and *always* communicate."

Other SE teams suggest a good division of labor. Patsy Hennin of the Shelter Institute says that working with her husband ". . . is wonderful. We're very different, very independent, very individual. We divided up the business so we don't get in each other's way. That way our talents complement each other."

Not all SE's, however, are as certain as the Hennins or the Kays. Barbara Brabec, author of two books on running home businesses and publisher of the *National Home Business Report* (See SE Library, Section I), started her business with her husband as an equal partner, but chose to shake up the organizational chart. According to Brabec, "Both of us wanted to be boss, and you can't run a business like that. Since Harry had a full-time job and I was the expert on the project, we decided I would run the business and Harry would work for me. I think you really need a strong marriage to stand up against the kind of situation we've been living with. We found that we had to strike a good balance between the marriage and the business, but many couples, unfortunately, don't."

The moral of these stories? Make an honest assessment of your marriage before you attempt working together as business partners. Weigh the risks carefully before extending the marriage vows to include "till profits do us part."

4. *Make sure all potential partners share your goals.* Most partnerships collapse because the people involved have different goals. Some may want to build up a business quickly, window-dress it, then sell it. Others may want to develop it as a lifelong enterprise. Still others may want to see it spin off in new directions and shed old divisions. As Marilyn Dashe says, "You have to have a clear understanding about what everyone wants from the start, especially about money and division of labor. Once the business develops, it's hard to go back and change track."

Master Hui went on to tell of the famous General Kao Ling: "Kao's troops were so feared that often his enemies would lay down their weapons and surrender at the sight of Kao's approaching banner. Once, while enlisting warriors in a small village, Kao made it known he was looking for skilled fighters. A dozen youths grabbed sticks, hoes, and other tools and vigorously demonstrated their prowess on fences, trees, and each other. When they had finished their display, Kao smiled and sent the exhausted young men home, and then enlisted five youths who had simply stood watching the fray."

"Why did he do that?"asked Shen Ti. "I would think that such a demonstration of strength and enthusiasm would surely impress a fighting man."

"Kao looked at the five who stood quietly through the chaos and knew they shared his fundamental belief: the great swordsman does not live his life with blade drawn. There was nothing to fight, so they did not do battle. They shared his understanding and thereby earned the right to fight at his side."

It's all in the family. In 1983 three sisters-in-law, Kitty, Sharon, and Shoreh Shadman, and a neighbor-friend, Rebecca Durfee (Rockville, MD), decided to conduct the acid test of human relationships by going into business together. It was an interesting mix of backgrounds and skills: Kitty had taught public school, Sharon directed a day-care center, Shoreh sold real estate, and Rebecca had been a retail buyer. The four women figured their combined interests spelled selling merchandise and teaching kids, so they pooled their experience with a growing interest in computers to form a novel business, Computer Kids. The store is a perfect example of Techno Age thinking in action, combining a retail computer sales operation with a school that teaches families how to put computers to productive use.

After thoroughly researching their idea, the four women began to realize the problems of divvying up the responsibilities. Not only did each one bring different skills to the enterprise, but each had contributed a different amount of capital. To make matters even more complicated, all four husbands had also invested. "At the beginning it was really rocky," says Rebecca Durfee. "When the responsibilities weren't delegated, we were stepping all over each other's toes. And in a close-knit family situation, that can get very tense."

To resolve the responsibility issue, each woman now controls a single aspect of the business. Rebecca handles software purchasing, Sharon manages staffing, Kitty does marketing and publicity, and Shoreh keeps the books. While the partners carefully keep communication lines open, they strive to remain sensitive to each other's roles and autonomy.

The equality issue was much more difficult to resolve. The four partners decided to form a board of directors that included their husbands. The votes of each member of the board reflected his or her contribution of time and/or money. So while the partners do not have equal voting power, they do have votes equal to sweat equity and capital investment. While establishing the voting method produced a certain amount of tension, it now seems to be working smoothly.

One might think that family members working together would produce an intolerable amount of awkwardness and hard feelings. Kitty Shadman, however, disagrees. "The fears of the business world were somewhat lessened because we have a common bond," she says. "If things get rough we'll stick together. We complement each other, and because of our relationship, we feel comfortable with each other."

While commitment is crucial in a partnership, Durfee stresses flexibility. "The family gets along really well to begin with," she says, "but that's nothing if people insist on being stubborn. In this case, no one's ego interferes with decision-making or policy making. And that's a real benefit."

Now that Computer Kids has navigated the rough waters, the four women anticipate inevitable success. According to Kitty, their projected annual income will be "Millions!" While her answer may have been slightly tongue-in-cheek, there is no question that such enthusiasm has helped give birth to a family success story.

CREATING A STRONG STRUCTURE

With money in hand and partners on board (or not), you still can't move forward without some sort of formal business structure. Many would-be entrepreneurs run out and incorporate the day after they get an idea, only to find that the business doesn't make sense, and they end up with a non-income-generating shell that requires administrative coddling and (in states like Massachusetts) saddles you with annual excise taxes.

Before selecting a structure, SE's always take liability and tax benefits into account. Let's take a brief look at liabilities that can dampen if not destroy any creative endeavor. If there's a chance, no matter how slim, that you can be held personally liable if something goes wrong, you'll probably want to incorporate because doing so shelters your personal assets whenever your company gets sued. (It won't, however, protect you from the slammer if you knowingly commit illegal or fraudulent business transactions.) Such liability protection can be important in this era of windfall court decisions where everyone seems to be suing everyone else.

While this trend may depress you, don't let the threat of litigation paralyze you. Instead, visit an attorney *who specializes in small businesses* to discuss your "exposure"—what you or your business might be sued for when dealing with other people and

other business entities. He or she can advise you on incorporation, design solid contracts with clients and customers to provide
maximum protection, and advise you whether you need professional liability insurance.

Most incorporation papers are boilerplate, as are the "by-
laws" (detailed and arcane gibberish spelling out the fine points
of what your company and its officers can and cannot do). In
fact, if your incorporation is routine, you can save yourself some
money by consulting two Enterprise publications: *How to Form
Your Own Corporation Without a Lawyer for Under $50* by Ted
Nichols and *The Basic Book of Business Agreements* by Arnold
Goldstein (see SE Library, Section I). If, on the other hand, you
have partners and complicated "buy-out" agreements, you're
best off letting your lawyer do the dirty work.

How much should you rely on an attorney? While lawyers
might argue that no one should cross the street without consulting one of their brethren, common sense will keep you out of
more trouble than all the legal eagles in Washington. Attorney
Bruce Sunstein, who has counseled numerous Soft-Skilled Entrepreneurs, suggests that once you've established some routine
ways of doing business, you really don't need a lawyer for anything but special situations. "Entrepreneurship by definition
means undertaking something new, and in most cases the entrepreneur will be doing something for which he has little prior
training. So it's worth hiring a specialist to take care of basics,
like doing business with the outside world, hiring people, bringing in technology, contracts, and the like. Once your business has
gained its footing, you can become more comfortable about
making decisions on your own. In any case, don't shy away from
good legal planning in the beginning—it can save you a lot of
grief when you least need it."

As for taxes, start off with a good accountant experienced
with small businesses. While your friendly family accountant
may have learned a few things in accounting school, you'll want
someone who knows every subtle trick and keeps up with the
ever-changing tax laws.

Like attorneys, accountants can help you most in the beginning. Even if liability isn't an issue, some form of incorporation
may still make sense, in light of certain tax savings and perks that
offset the cost of maintaining them. It's also wise to have the ac-

countant (or an assistant) set up your books and teach you how to
maintain them yourself. After that, don't rely on an accountant
unless absolutely necessary. Watch how the various tax forms are
filled out, and ask questions so you can take care of them yourself
on the next filing. There's no reason to farm out simple fifteen-
minute paperwork at top dollar. A good accounting firm will
always be willing to let you do the routine work, merely looking
over your shoulder to make sure you do it right.

In any case, the SE's motto when dealing with lawyers, accountants, and other consultants is this: "I look, I learn, then I do
for myself."

OTHER START-UP DOLLAR SAVERS

Throughout this chapter you've seen the importance of
thinking lean, bartering, and substituting creative thought and
energy for dollars whenever possible. Remember, any money you
don't spend on overhead is either money saved or money you can
put behind a better product or service. The following checklist
can further help you keep your start-up costs to a bare minimum:

1. *Furnishings and fixtures.* If you don't need to impress clients or customers, go for the cheapest makeshift items you can
find. If you need an impressive façade, you can often get practically new furnishings for a song at bankruptcy auctions (from
people who spent too much initially) or from used-office-
equipment dealers.

2. *Telephone.* Don't get conned into buying a fancy electronic system with a forty-station intercom and paging system. It
will only clutter up your garage or kitchen. Get the cheapest system with the fewest lines. Many electronic stores sell add-on giz-
mos that can embellish a phone system. What about the future?
When you get to the point where you need a more sophisticated
system, you'll also be in a better position to buy it outright or
lease it.

3. *Insurance.* Like taxes, insurance is a necessary evil. But
unlike taxes, you have to take care of it only once. It's worth sitting down with an insurance agent *who handles other small business accounts.* Find out about umbrella plans that cover all your

present and future needs, and compare them with buying bits and pieces of insurance from different underwriters.

In any event, try to get exactly as much property insurance as you need. Underinsurance can be costly, and overinsurance can waste money. Buy what seems sensible, increasing the coverage as your needs change. If you think you'll be buying some expensive equipment in a year, wait until you're actually ready to make the purchase before upping your coverage.

Other than theft insurance, you might want to look into a health-insurance policy for you and your partners and employees. Rather than buying through an insurance agent, first check with your chamber of commerce to see if they have any health-insurance programs for small businesses. If not, contact regional small business associations, which usually offer good group rates (shop around—the rates vary among organizations).

4. *Basic supplies*. Buy what you need as you need it. True, you may pay a higher unit price, but getting a great price on 400 boxes of number-two pencils and 50,000 envelopes isn't going to help you build up a customer/client base and survive the tough times.

5. *A computer*. If you believed all the computer ads in magazines and on television, you'd wonder how you manage to get out of bed without a program to activate your brain. An essential small investment, the ads tell you. In reality, not so small: to do any kind of useful business work, you're going to have to shell out or commit yourself to between $2,000 and $4,000 for decent hardware and *useful* software. And unless your business absolutely demands computerization from the start, a computer will probably collect more dust than your old Pong game.

First of all, if you don't know how to use a computer, it will take anywhere from three weeks to three months of dedicated effort to put it to productive use, time you could better spend developing or marketing your goods or service. Second, manual checkwriting and accounting systems developed for small businesses (such as the one manufactured by Safeguard) serve most start-ups quite well. Many a seven-digit company has survived for years using them.

Finally, a computer can actually become a smokescreen for serious management problems that fifteen different reports and graphs won't solve. The bottom line is this: small businesses did well before the advent of microcomputers and they'll continue to do so in the computer age. If you have a computer now and can press it into service, fine. If not, don't worry about it. You can take pride in sailing through the Techno Age with typewriter, pencil, and calculator.

EXERCISE 5: ENTREPRENOPOLY

Few things cause stronger reactions in previously level-headed people than the prospect of making or losing a lot of money. Before you seriously approach friends or family for OPEC, you might want to test their true reactions by proposing a little game of Entreprenopoly.

Take the money from a Monopoly set or print denominations on scraps of paper. Sit everyone down around the kitchen table and divide the funny money equally. Then propose an investment scheme, something silly or outrageous, such as a company that manufactures butcher-block kitty-litter boxes or an enterprise that markets solar-powered can openers. Who wants to invest? Collect all the money, then either double it or light a match to it. How do the investors react? Try it again using your secret SE project. It's only a game, but you'll see some unexpected reactions. Friendships have been destroyed by what started out as a "friendly" game; how much more damage can a life-and-death SE game do?

6
MARKETING YOUR IDEA: HOW TO HIT THE BULL'S-EYE

An unseasonably icy wind ripped across the valley in early spring, forcing Master Hui's disciples indoors, where they could scarcely keep warm because they had burned most of their fuel during the long winter.

The disciples agreed to take turns tending the small fire, warming themselves in turn while their companions sought the internal warmth of meditation. As Master Hui passed the stove one day, he noticed that Shen Ti had carefully separated the coals after they had begun to glow, and asked for an explanation.

"Fuel can be transformed into heat," Shen Ti said. "The closer you pack the coals, the more heat they produce. But the hotter the fire, the more fuel it consumes. It is therefore best to do with less heat."

Master Hui nodded in agreement and raised his own hands to the stove. "He who enjoys plentiful fuel often squanders it. The wise man knows the value of conserving his fuel even in times of plenty. In such a way, he never risks freezing."

BORN SALESPEOPLE

Realize it or not, all of us sell something with almost every breath we take. Unfortunately, ever since Willie Loman gave "selling" a bad name, many of us have preferred to ignore the "sales pitches" we make every day. Think about your own life for a moment. Did you recently persuade a friend or spouse to go to a particular movie you wanted to see? Have you ever had to convince a child to eat a helping of spinach, a teacher to grant an extension on a paper, or a boss to award you a raise? At the very least, you've talked yourself into getting out of bed when your alarm went off. Persuading, convincing, justifying, and talking ourselves and others into certain beliefs and actions all involve selling. If you've done any of these things, you've drawn from a rich supply of tacit marketing skills you may have always taken for granted.

This chapter will enable you to consciously harness such tacit marketing skills to your SE project. It reveals five different approaches to selling any product, whether it's yourself, an idea, a publication, a service, or a widget. Many of these techniques can also be used to present ideas and fortify your position within an organization.

For each approach you'll learn the advantages and pitfalls, as well as step-by-step advice on implementing them. Even if you're already a super salesperson, you'll probably benefit from the section on obtaining free media exposure. By the end of the chapter, you'll be able to draw up a marketing strategy ideally suited to your particular project and skills.

PREREQUISITES TO MARKETING 101

A great marketing plan depends on three key elements: commitment, understanding, and readiness. Commitment means *believing* in what you're doing, standing behind it 110 percent even when the road turns rocky. It means becoming a fanatic, fueled by a burning desire to persuade and convince the world to share in your faith. When you commit yourself fully to a project, you automatically become a successful promoter of it. As literary agent Michael Snell emphasizes, "An ounce of passion will transform even the most shy and inarticulate person into a world-class salesperson."

The second key element, a thorough understanding of your product, also makes selling easy. With your keen awareness of its every detail, you will be able to explain fully what it does, detail exactly who should buy it, and demonstrate why it beats the pants off the competition. Understanding your product will help you anticipate all conceivable objections and design airtight arguments to knock them down. In fact, good salespeople actually elicit objections from their prospects and use them to close a deal. As supersalesman Jeff Strauss recommends, "Once you get people talking about why they don't want your product or why they prefer someone else's, you're only a breath away from convincing them that they really aren't totally satisfied with their present situation and that you're offering a much better alternative." To make that leap, you must know your product—inside and out.

Readiness is the third prerequisite to a successful marketing campaign. Few mistakes will kill a campaign faster than not having the product ready to ship when promised, or, even worse, shipping an incomplete product that you must later recall and repair.

Take a lesson from the software industry, which seems bent on setting a record for premature product releases. Many small software developers suffer such paranoia about being scooped by competitors that they distribute hasty and faulty versions of their work. Customers complain, the computer magazines pan the programs, and word-of-mouth soon spreads that the programs are full of "bugs." Even though the software entrepreneur may eventually clean up the product, he or she must overcome one of the deadliest obstacles of all: a bad reputation.

Premature marketers also court legal problems if they accept money for a product they can't deliver. The Federal Trade Commission dictates tight rules concerning product availability, and each state polices its own consumer-protection laws. As one SE sums it up, "Never stick it to the public, because they'll stick it right back to you. And they don't forget. Once you've been branded as a bad egg, you'll waste a lot of time selling your credibility rather than your product."

THE SOFT-SKILLED MARKETEER

To understand the basic structure of the SE approach to marketing, visualize a target. The bull's-eye represents the ultimate SE achievement: selling your goods through no-cost/low-cost P.R. and promotion techniques. The next ring in the target represents grass-roots marketing efforts in which you begin selling your product to friends and relatives before expanding to the surrounding community, and the third ring begins to include more people through a technique popularly known as "networking" (building relationships with people and organizations to extend your own capabilities). Moving outward to the fourth ring, we encounter direct-mail advertising, which can reach very large definable audiences. The final ring, paid advertising, is the most powerful and, as we'll see later, the most perilous form of marketing you can undertake.

Before we consider the five approaches in more detail, bear in mind that a good marketing campaign may use one or more in a variety of proportions and combinations. The goal, however, always remains the same: attracting other people's money without spending too much of your own.

THE CENTER RING: THE ULTIMATE ADVERTISING BARGAIN

A conventional seller of high-fashion maternity clothes would buy a full-page ad in *Woman's Day* magazine, but an SE would convince an editor of the magazine to publish a three-page article about her revolutionary designs. While the traditional seller of an elite dating service for business travelers might buy a spot on daytime television, an SE would be a guest on the Phil Donahue show. Such "free media" not only costs you nothing (or very little) but also does not arouse the suspicions of a public that has grown increasingly skeptical of the barrage of advertising that bombards it every day.

Political candidates rely so heavily on free media that they hire full time press secretaries to write press releases with which they blanket newspapers and television networks. You might think of an SE marketing campaign as a political battle to sell your product.

Many SE's cited throughout this book have exploited free media. Warren Holland, creator of the Decipher game (Chapter 4), so tantalized the media that he was able to obtain press coverage that gave him the equivalent of an expensive national advertising campaign. In fact, Holland managed to succeed with a marketing budget of zero. While it's difficult to use free media to that extent, many of the entrepreneurs cited so far, including Frieda Yamins of Italia Adagio, Wally Amos, creator of the Famous Amos chocolate chip cookie, and the Bergstroms, founders of the Toybrary, have all used good press coverage to get their products out of their kitchens or basements and into customers' hands. How can you get the same kind of coverage?

1. *Make your project newsworthy.* An effective press release will tell the world about your project. But unless your idea is outlandish, flashy, or very timely, a mere description of it may get you nothing more than yawns from editors. Find an angle that will grab people by the lapels and rattle their teeth. Tweezerman Dal La Magna hired a P.R. firm that used the absurdity of a Harvard MBA selling tweezers to attract the attention of a *Forbes* editor. Then La Magna turned the sad fact that he had not made money until then into a joke by calculating that he had singlehandedly lowered the average income of his Harvard class by $80 per person.

Try to cite an interesting fact, a startling statistic or phenomenon about your industry that will hopefully spark the interest of a journalist or editor. For instance, if you're running an information-retrieval service, include in your press release hard numbers about how much time and money various types of businesses can save by retrieving information electronically. Your company may be only a small part of the resulting story, but publication in a major national periodical will give you a tremendous credibility boost.

When you put together a press release, make sure you: 1) Use the standard format that most media professionals have adopted for business use. In the upper corner, put the date the release is written, the date that the information is to be disseminated (if immediately, put "For immediate release"), and the contact's name and phone number. Double-space the release, keeping it within two pages at most—a press release will be scanned, not studied. 2) Use short sentences, short paragraphs, and numerous facts and figures. Save your full sales pitch for another forum. 3) Include a headline that engagingly summarizes the point of the release. 4) Make it easy for a reporter, editor, or

producer to respond to your release without any further information. Answer the journalistic basics—who, what, why, when,
where, and how.

2. *Get inside the media.* A good press release will never
make news unless it gets to the right people. Assemble a press list
from one of the standard directories listed in the SE Library (Section III). Such a press list should include newspapers, magazines,
and TV and radio stations. When dealing with newspapers and
magazines, make sure you've targeted the right editors: a press
release describing your breakthrough in odorless dog food will
have little appeal to the editor of the automotive section.

Despite the best efforts at targeting a list, the chances of any
press release actually getting read are slim, because every other
would-be entrepreneur and celebrity is also clamoring for free
media. The solution? *Better* targeting and follow-up. You can
improve your chances by sending your release to people in the
media who *have a demonstrated interest in your particular field*,
rather than gambling that an editor will farm it out to them. If
you notice that a staff writer for *The Wall Street Journal* constantly writes about educational software, and you've just started
marketing a unique software "sampler" for schools, fire off a
press release to that person immediately.

Follow up your release with a phone call to check on interest
in your project, reminding the reporter that your work ties in
nicely with his or her interests. Even if the reporter doesn't write
your story, he or she might use you later as a resource for another
article. Danielle Torrez, founder of a modeling school in Boston,
made friends with a gossip columnist for a local paper. Whenever
something interesting happens to Danielle or her business, she
gets immediate coverage in the gossip or fashion pages. Torrez
recommends, however, that you choose your "media alliances"
carefully, so you can control the way information about you is
used and distributed.

The closer you can get to people, the better your chances of
getting good coverage when you need it. Ken Lizotte is a professional author and journalist in Boston who has deftly used the
media to promote his work as a free-lance writer. Lizotte advises
that you ". . . get to know the newspeople by socializing with
them. Find out where they hang out. Then present yourself as an
expert in a particular field, so that you're one of the first people

they call when a story breaks." You can create an ideal situation, Lizotte observes, when you develop such strong rapport with media people that you can hand-deliver a press release to a contact and ". . . pretty much guarantee ink when you need it."

3. *Sponsor a special event and invite the media.* Newspeople can always be enticed to cover events if they're given a good lure. If you have an astonishing new widget, invite celebrities to an interesting place for a demonstration. If you run an unusual service, give a free demonstration, seminar, or training session. Turn a normal session into a big splash. That's what Linda Gregg and Laurel Gruenwald did with Interpersonal Software, the company that arranges gatherings for women who want to learn about computers and software. Gregg and Gruenwald have invited hundreds of press people to their sessions, and the effort has paid off in valuable television, radio, and newspaper coverage.

There are numerous offshoots of this tactic, some of which have been used for years by shrewd entrepreneurs. Take the case of Elisha Graves Otis, who in the 1850's invented the elevator. Otis found himself up against a public that believed only freight was meant to be hauled up on hoists. To demonstrate that people could be safely carried into the sky too, he set up a demonstration at the first World's Fair, held in New York City. Otis himself climbed aboard his "safety hoist" and was whisked away. Then he had an assistant *cut the rope* holding up the hoist. A teeth-gritting public and press watched in amazement as the world's first safety elevator and its inventor remained in the air. That event ushered in the age of elevators and launched the billion-dollar Otis Elevator Company.

Of more recent vintage, two years ago there was a turkey—a wild turkey—on the White House lawn. No one knew how it got there, but it gobbled in front of tens of millions of people who watched the evening news. The media speculated that the incident was staged by the advertising agency of the company that sells Wild Turkey bourbon. Though the company denied any such action, it received extensive name recognition that would have cost hundreds of thousands of dollars in paid advertising to achieve the same result. While you might not want to tangle with turkeys in Washington, you can imagine how a wild P.R. stunt could potentially give you a lot of mileage for very little money.

You can also obtain excellent free advertising whenever you accept a speaking engagement, be it at the local Rotary Club, a cross-town college, or an industry conference. Here's how to make this mode of free advertising work for you:

1. *Get yourself onto the speaker's platform.* Talking before a group of people establishes your expertise and promotes your project at the same time. Let's say you're setting up a new word-processing service. One way to announce your existence might be to contact a local business association, promising that you have valuable inside information about how any business can get the most for its money from using outside word processing. You might also suggest that the association's members would profit from hearing such information, and that you'd be glad to speak at one of their meetings. The payoff to you is obvious: once you gain confidence about speaking at small local events, you can tackle larger organizations and even national gatherings.

A living example of the efficacy of this technique is Dr. Jeffrey Lant, who has written numerous self-published books on consulting, including *The Unabashed Self-Promoter's Guide* (see SE Library, Section III). Lant has managed to get himself recommended for just about every conceivable kind of speaking engagement, and in doing so has made his books and consulting services nationally known.

2. *Get yourself invited to radio and TV talk shows.* Mass media allow you to display your knowledge and expertise to a vast audience, but first you must convince station hosts and producers that you will make an exciting guest. Ken Lizotte suggests starting off small, through cable TV: "Cable TV is a fabulous way to get free exposure now, because there are so many cable stations sprouting up around the country, and they're just aching for interesting guests. I knew of an author who wrote a book, but his publisher hadn't given him much promotional money. So he packed five hundred copies in the trunk of his car and spent an entire summer traveling cross-country, presenting himself to the media all along the way. The book took off like a rocket."

3. *Teach a course or seminar at an adult-education center.* Many SE's launch a project by teaching a course at night. Everyone comes out a winner: the students benefit from your expertise

at a bargain rate, and you get to advertise yourself and get paid at the same time. Marilyn Dashe, who formerly taught English and now runs a technical writing service, says: "We now use teaching for support—it really gives us free advertising. If you stand in front of twenty-five new people for a day, then twenty-five more people know about you."

4. *Write an article or book about your area of expertise.* Finally, you can get your name in print by writing an article yourself. To get your piece published and read, you should provide little-known or fascinating facts about your field, offer a solution to a major problem, praise or lament the state of the art, give timely insights that relate your field to current headlines, summarize the essential dos and don'ts for novices, or forecast where the field will be in five years. Submit the article to the publication that is most suited to the subject matter and the level of exposure you desire (see the SE Library, Section III, for media directories).

How does this kind of free advertising work? Pretend you're SE Russell Smith, who raises ferrets. To increase public awareness that ferrets make great pets, you write an article describing the virtues of owning one of the furry beasts, touting them as the ultimate urban companion. You also provide insights into proper care and feeding. At the end of the article you include your own interesting story, which of course promotes your own Ferret Barrel. If the article were printed in the life-style section of a medium- to large-sized newspaper or a Sunday magazine, you'd probably enjoy an immediate increase in inquiries and sales. Again, it's a win-win situation: the public learns something new, while your business gets a boost.

Like an article, a book can be a powerful calling card. Attorney Arnold Goldstein, for example, wrote *How to Save Your Business*, an essential guide to avoiding bankruptcy. Although it sold only a few thousand copies and yielded small royalties, it churned up $300,000 in legal and consulting fees. Again, you can ride a flood of ink down the river of success.

Not everyone has the time and stamina to write a book, but many small businesses do print brochures about their goods or services. Typically these sell the product or service directly, but you can sometimes get better results with an indirect pitch. The Ferret Barrel could hype its own products or sell the "idea" of ferrets. Similarly, a company that manufactures solar collectors could talk about the advantages of its own products or discuss the concepts of good solar design in general. While product- and company-specific brochures are important, also consider educating the public about your field. Such subtle advertising may ultimately be more acceptable and garner you more sales or contracts than conventional routes.

There is an infinite number of creative ways to advertise your product or service with nothing but an investment of your time and ingenuity.

One morning Master Hui hid the remaining fuel. "Shen Ti,"
he said, "we have consumed the last of the fuel. What do you
propose now?"
Shen Ti shivered. "I could burn my coat or the thatches of
the roof, but that would provide only temporary warmth, and I
would eventually feel the cold wind even more. However, we do
have plenty of rice."
"You would burn the rice for fuel?"
"No, I will inform our gossipy neighbor that we will trade a
good deal of surplus rice for a small amount of kindling and a
few logs. Perhaps someone in the village has plenty of fuel but
not enough food."

He left the corporation—and lived to tell about it. "I saw a steady stream of young, aggressive MBA types joining the ranks," recalls Neil Duane (Auburn, MA), "and it dawned on me that I could be put out to pasture someday." So after ten years of working his way up to become the manager of two technical writing departments at the prestigious computer firm of Hewlett Packard, Duane cleaned out his desk and struck out on his own to start Boston Documentation Design. Later, four other former employees joined him in his endeavor.

Duane attributes much of his eventual success to the contacts he made during his early days at HP, when he taught night courses in Boston University's science communication program. Says Duane, "About one-third of the people in the program were sent there by their employers, most of whom were in the high-tech field. People liked my courses, so they'd go back and tell their superiors about me. This had a tremendous positive effect on my reputation both as a teacher and as an expert. One time a student's boss called me up to ask about estimating the cost of producing computer manuals. I gave her a mini course and then realized that lots of other managers must have the same questions. So I worked up an advanced version of my basic cost-estimating lecture and arranged to give it to fifty managers at once. Through sessions like that I came to know nearly everyone in the industry."

In addition to providing him with a rich supply of business contacts, that intimacy with the field has made Duane a star: he's constantly asked to review books, sit on panels, and speak at gatherings of technical writers. Each event gives him and his new company more visibility and credibility. Says Duane, "None of my speaking or teaching activities really pay much, but that's not the point. To succeed in my field you have to practice what you do well, teach others, and take the time to make some contribution to the profession. The total rewards are far greater than the sum of the parts and will continue for many years into your career."

THE FIRST RING: GRASS-ROOTS MARKETING

For the Soft-Skilled Entrepreneur, grass-roots marketing not only test-drives products and sales pitches but also helps generate the money and recognition needed to launch a more ambitious campaign. Many SE's begin by giving away or discounting a product to friends and relatives, refining both the product and the sales pitch as they assess the feedback they hear. Next they take the new, improved product to local stores and, based on feedback from the storeowners or customers, further refine the product or its packaging. When no more objections crop up, they present their product to the store's distributor, who might be able to pump it into the national distribution pipeline.

Charles Hornsby (Brattleboro, VT) used exactly this method to turn a flair for baking French bread into a lucrative enterprise. After Hornsby was laid off from his job as an international student-travel administrator, he and his wife decided to stay in Vermont and risk unemployment rather than move to an area less to their liking. Having received rave reviews from friends and relatives for their homemade French bread, the Hornsbys started baking twelve loaves a day. Their friends eagerly purchased each day's results and offered valuable suggestions for perfecting the product. With new, improved loaves in hand, the Hornsbys approached several local supermarkets, which began carrying limited quantities. Within six months the bread was selling well enough for the Hornsbys to begin setting up their own delivery routes, eventually winning "Baguette Bakery" distribution throughout the six New England states. Because of their success they were later able to add croissants and frozen garlic bread to their line.

Richard Motta, creator of the world-famous Chipwich, played a sweet variation on this theme. For years Motta had delighted his friends with a dessert delicacy consisting of a layer of ice cream sandwiched between two large chocolate chip cookies and coated with chocolate syrup. Dubbing it the Chipwich, Motta decided to start selling his product seriously, but he sidestepped conventional stores and hired clean-cut kids to hawk his product from pushcarts on the streets of Manhattan. The idea came to him when he saw fleets of croissant pushcarts doing excellent business. Motta's own pushcart sales skyrocketed, enabling him to mass-produce his Chipwiches, sign on with a distributor, and create a booming international market for himself.

Foodstuffs aren't the only kinds of products that can benefit from a grass-roots marketing campaign; other SE projects, services, and widgets can easily gain a foothold this way. SE Ikuku

Atsumi, for example, launched the New England Japanese Center by traveling through Massachusetts' High-Tech Belt to discuss the difficulties American firms encounter when conducting business with Japan. The Center now provides those same firms with "cultural consultation," technical translations, and related services. SE Jill Fallon, the inventor of Walkabout historical tapes of Boston, began her enterprise by persuading local hotels and travel agencies to evaluate her demo tapes. Their response helped her shape a more ambitious marketing campaign. SE RoJean Loucks tested and refined her nursing-wear patterns by talking with all of the contacts she'd made through her local Nursing Mothers Association. And SE Rita Press, creator of Labeleze, got on the road to national distribution through supermarket chains in her own neighborhood.

As most SE's find, once a grass-roots campaign overcomes initial inertia and gets rolling, word-of-mouth turns it into a perpetual-motion machine. Cynthia Tate and Phyllis Newcomb of Clarion, Iowa, discovered this to be particularly true for their own venture, EduComp. Tate and Newcomb were looking for something to do while their children went to school. After deciding to go to college, they wound up taking computer and programming courses, but soon realized that a B.A. wasn't an automatic ticket to success in the business world. So they approached nearby public schools, offering to instruct teachers and employees about the PC's that the school board had just purchased. The schools jumped at their Techno Age–style proposal, and the two women immediately formed EduComp, which has since expanded to include PC training courses for adults and children on weekends, evenings, and during the summer.

Since Tate and Newcomb live and teach in a small farming community, their best form of advertising is word of mouth. "People around here started getting very curious about us," says Tate. " 'I hear you went to school in computers,' they'd say. 'We just bought one and need some help. Could you stop by?' I don't think a day goes by when someone doesn't ask a farm-related question about computers. The fact that we both come from farm families and run farms too really lends credibility to our enterprise. People trust us, so the word gets around."

Although the details of each grass-roots marketing plan will vary, most SE's agree on several major points:

1. *Be professional, no matter how humble the circum-stances.* Whether you're carting your first loaves of bread to nearby mom-and-pop stores or locally distributing brochures for a technical writing service, always pay attention to how profes-sionally you package your product and present yourself. While you don't have to waste a fortune on dressing up your product or yourself, you must spend whatever it takes to look good.

At the very least, spring for a business card and disguise yourself as a business person. Before you show storeowners sam-ples of your wares, make sure the packaging would not look out of place on their shelves. If you don't have any layout or design experience, barter your service or product with a graphic artist who can help you develop an attractive label, box, bag, or bro-chure. To locate competent graphic artists in your area, call local printers or typesetters to see whom they recommend. Browse through stores or catalogs, keeping alert for attractive packaging that you can copy.

Brochures and other literature should create the image you desire. While a typewritten piece may sometimes be adequate, typesetting always has a more professional aura. Here again, you might barter for the services of a graphic artist or typesetter. Re-member, you don't need a thousand-dollar logo, just a good clean look. Cambridge graphic designer Greg Wright, of Krueger Wright Design, who has helped many SE's design low-cost brochures, advises, "Keep it simple, know your audience, and speak in a language your audience can understand. Use the designer as your interpreter. Also, save yourself time and money by having your information organized and complete before en-gaging the graphic designer in the process."

2. *Give the impression that you're here to stay.* One prob-lem inherent in the grass-roots method is the tendency of poten-tial distribution outlets and clients to suspect that you're going to be just another flash in the pan. To put people's minds at rest, describe some of your future plans for the product as well as any spin-off projects you might have in the works. Potential cus-tomers, distributors, and clients always like to hear that you're thinking about tomorrow, pondering ways to improve your busi-ness. SE's Bob and Marianne Moran say that believing your busi-ness to be marching forward wins half the battle. As Bob puts it, "If you really think you're going places, you won't have to con-

vince others—you naturally radiate your belief, and that begins to affect others."

3. *Never let the turkeys get you down.* Not all grass-roots campaigns ignite like brushfires. Sometimes you must adjust your approach before your product begins to move. If a distributor or potential client turns you down, always ask how you can modify your goods or services to make them more appealing. Try to turn every objection into a learning experience.

Not all rejections, of course, will be rational. Just chalk those up to a world overpopulated with people who lack imagination. Many of the world's best-selling products or ideas prompt horselaughs, for, as Albert Einstein reportedly lamented, "Great spirits have always encountered violent opposition from mediocre minds."

Within a day the entire village knew of Shen Ti's offer to exchange rice for fuel, and the widow who lived down the road wished to make a trade. Master Hui was surprised, though, when Shen Ti returned from her house with kindling, logs, and the same sack of rice he had taken for barter. "Shen Ti," said the Master, "you did not trade the rice? And have you lost your bow?"

Shen Ti exposed his empty quiver. "The widow laughed at my offer of rice, saying it would feed her large family for only a week. So I taught her son to hunt and traded my bow and arrows for a week's worth of fuel."

Making a good clean buck. Jed Roth (Wellesley, MA) tossed out the textbook and redefined the term "car wash" to mean "total car care." As Roth sums it up: "We prepare the car, remove any scratches, tar, or oxidation, and buff it to bring back the showroom shine. Then we apply industrial-grade wax to protect what we've just done. We clean the bumpers, tires, chrome, glass, moldings, both inside and outside the car. We treat the upholstery or leather and run the carpets through a dirt-extraction machine. Anything else that needs to be done is done." At $125 per cleaning, Roth's service attracts elite customers who drive Porsches, Mercedeses, BMW's, and other expensive cars.

Roth started his business while still in college, plugging his cleaning machine into a dorm-room socket so he could spruce up his classmates' cars for $80 a shot. With expenses amounting to about $4 per car, Roth walked away from each job with a $76 profit. Amazed at such profitability, he formed Professional Car Care, then hit the road to solicit customers.

He began his local advertising campaign by perching himself on the hood of his own car in parking lots, stopping every imported auto he saw, and asking the drivers if they'd like to have their cars professionally cleaned. While this method generated good business, it didn't produce enough volume to satisfy the ambitious Roth.

So he began slapping his business cards on the windshields of all likely prospects in parking lots. The cards pulled in more customers, the business continued to thrive, but Roth soon found he could no longer waste time on parking-lot crusades. Furthermore, the added overhead costs involved in renting space for his company meant he needed more volume than ever. Drawing from his ready supply of daring creativity, Roth hired a crew of twelve-year-old boys to ride around parking lots on their bikes, dispensing cards, getting a five-dollar commission per customer. "You should have seen it!" exclaims Roth. "They could lay down the cards ten times faster than I ever could, and business grew by leaps and bounds. Some of the kids were making fifty dollars or more a day."

Although Roth next plans a direct-mail campaign, he will never pass up an opportunity to creatively market his service on a personal level: "I was driving down Main Street," Roth recalls, "and saw a Porsche parked on the curb in front of a small office building. I walked into the office and said to the secretary, 'Can I speak to the man who owns the green Porsche?' The secretary buzzed the owner and told him, 'There's someone here to see you about your car.' The guy must have thought to himself, 'Holy cow! Someone's hit my Porsche!' He flew down the elevator, ran out to the parking lot, tie flapping in the breeze, sweating like a bull. And I said, 'Hi. My name is Jed Roth and I was wondering if you'd like to get your car cleaned.' The guy was so relieved he signed right up."

THE SECOND RING: BUILDING NETWORKS

"Networking" is getting people and organizations to provide contacts that will help you achieve your goals. And while you might groan at the thought of another noun being pressed into service as a verb, networking can help you market your product. In fact, it may be the most popular technique among Soft-Skilled Entrepreneurs. Networking is also popular among job-hunters and career-changers.

Suppose you want to land a job with IBM. You've even gotten an interview by responding to a newspaper ad. The interview goes well, and you're invited back for a second round. You can almost smell the ink drying on your first paycheck when the interviewer says, "Sorry, but we had so many applicants, the decision was tough. Unfortunately, you were our number-*two* candidate." What would you do in this situation? Pray for the number-one candidate to accept an offer from Wang instead? Write the interviewer a follow-up letter begging him to consider you for any other slots that open up in the future?

Such approaches may honor conventional textbook wisdom but would probably leave you at a dead end. Let's say you had your heart set on a technical-writing assignment at a major computer company. You'd ask the documentation manager at IBM if he: belongs to any professional associations; knows managers at other computer companies; or would let you get leads from his present staff, most of whom will have worked for one or more other companies. If your efforts obtain the names of the president of a local tech-writing association and four other documentation managers, plus five leads from staff ("Hey, call Bob Smith at DEC, he's looking for someone to fill my old job!"), you've got your first ten. Get ten from those ten, and you've expanded your range to one hundred possibilities.

The same principles help SE's locate clients or sales prospects. If a person or business you've contacted doesn't buy what you're selling, ask for ten names of people who might. The networking SE never leaves a marketing call empty-handed. SE Ken Lizotte discovered this principle in the early days of building up his business-writing service. "About fifty percent of my initial work came from people who *didn't* want to hire me," he recalls. "I always pushed for 'friends-of-friends' leads before hanging up the phone—those last few minutes were the most fruitful part of my marketing calls."

Leads are the building blocks of a successful business. Every new name is a prospective sale, an additional subscriber, a potential investor. Making an effective tool from these leads is a very personal and creative process. Barbara Brabec says, "You have to develop your own special network very early in the game. In my case, this meant sending hundreds of letters every year just to get acquainted with people I thought might *possibly* be interested in what I was doing. A lot of letters went unanswered but every so often I struck paydirt in the form of a valuable contact."

Like grass-roots marketing, networking requires innovation and imagination. The following five-point program will help you begin your own multiplication table:

1. *Make a personal inventory of everyone you know.* This might seem like an overwhelming task, but most people find it stimulating once they gain momentum. List all the personal, social, and professional contacts you've made in the past three years. You'll quickly find yourself remembering important people you forgot you knew, such as the grandmother you met at a cocktail party who bragged about her grandson's new job as vice-president of accounting for a major manufacturer of pharmaceuticals (and you've just invented a new phone-sanitizing aerosol spray!). Remember, for each name you add to your list, concentrate on ways to wring ten more names from that contact.

Jack Rochester developed an interesting way of expanding his inventory of contacts: "One day I sat down and decided to see how many names and associations I could list. So I set up an exercise for myself in which I'd pick a name and match a face to it. Then I'd imagine all the different contexts in which I'd heard that name or seen that face. At the end I had a list of more than one hundred people who could conceivably be part of my network. Five years later I still haven't exhausted the supply."

2. *Heighten your awareness of the networking potential in every new person you meet.* Every time you meet a new person, ask questions, not only about that person but also about his or her friends and associates. Most people like to talk about themselves and to brag about all the important people they know, so

you'll also gain a reputation as an excellent party or dinner guest, which, in turn, will increase your networking opportunities.

Many seasoned SE's advise that you follow up any encounter with a letter, a phone call, a date for a drink, or some other gesture that will cement your image in the other person's mind. After all, you want to become a part of his or her network, too. Barbara Brabec, for example, goes one step further to keep her name on the tip of her customers' tongues by personalizing her mailings. "Most of the time, my printed literature takes care of the request for information. Often though, I've felt compelled to include a small note, just a word of encouragement, a yes-or-no answer to a question, or perhaps even a lengthy letter. Now, several years later, I can really see the value of having written those thousands of little notes and letters."

3. *Draw on common bonds.* Network building often requires getting in touch with people you've never met but with whom you have something in common. That's why your college alumni magazine or the profiles of people in your local newspaper make such marvelous networking resources. People whose exploits and adventures, books and articles, promotions and honors deserve publicity usually appreciate the value of networking. If you start a new SE project, publish an article or book, or reach a milestone in your business, then immediately inform your alumni office and local newspaper while the "news" is still hot. You'll be amazed at how many new contacts you make.

If you cannot take advantage of the college bond, you can find other, equally useful sources, such as associations, clubs, community groups, school groups, and any other organization where people get together to share their interests.

Another approach is to start your own club, as Cambridge's Carol Verburg did. Ostensibly a Wednesday-night gathering at a local pub for aspiring fiction writers, Verburg's literary network seldom limited its discussions to Joyce Carol Oates. In fact, as a result of the networking that occurred, four writers landed lucrative ghostwriting assignments through an agent/member, two got software documentation jobs with computer companies, and one became a senior editor at a prestigious publishing house.

Other SE's have likewise benefited from networks that they helped establish. Irene Smalls, for example, orchestrated the weekly meetings of the "Friday Network," a group of entrepreneurs that met at a local restaurant to exchange information. The result was a wealth of valuable ideas and contacts for all the participants.

Finally, starting your own networking group provides a great opportunity for getting expert advice on business topics. Jane Frank founded a local entrepreneurs' network that meets once a month to swap contacts and bring in guest speakers. Over the course of three months, her group brought in professionals to speak on computers, taxes, and financial planning. The cost? Nothing. The speakers were all too glad to make new contacts and potential clients themselves.

4. *Join organizations outside your immediate area of expertise.* Peter Kinder tells the story of a young attorney who joined three exclusive country clubs to meet people and build up his practice. Sound textbook advice, of course, because so many of the other club members were lawyers or other professionals. After a year the young attorney had reduced his golf handicap, but he had won no new clients. So the next year he joined a T'ai Chi group, members of which eventually helped him build up a half-million-dollar-a-year practice.

As this lawyer discovered, it can be well worth your while to join associations or clubs whose members don't necessarily share your skills. For example, if you're a medical writer, try joining an association of nurses, laboratory directors, or other health-care workers who need to publish but may lack the professional writing abilities you can offer. Concentrate on large organizations that issue newsletters or magazines. If they accept your articles, it not only advertises your skills but also provides a ready opportunity for contacting people whose names appear in the publications. Again, the idea is to draw on a common bond.

Say your specialty is cactus gardening, and you join a horticultural society to make new contacts. You write an article on the synthesis of desert growing techniques, and you manage to get it published in the society's bimonthly magazine. After the magazine comes out, you've got an excellent reason for getting in touch with other people who published in the same issue. Strike up a conversation with the one who wrote about a new organic insecticide imported from Japan, and you just might pick up the name of the woman in Tokyo who will buy your freeze-dried cactus seeds.

5. *Review your networking files every few months.* SE's are only as strong as their information, and strong information must be current as well as complete. People move, and their jobs and interests change. If you haven't been in touch with someone in your file for six months, rekindle the contact to update your file. Aside from the pleasure you might get from catching up with old acquaintances, you might find a wealth of new ideas and opportunities at the other end of the phone. You might imitate Mike Snell and Ken Lizotte, who each month collect quotes and cartoons relevant to their work, then paste up and photocopy as many as one hundred double-sided sheets. For the price of the postage, they use these inexpensive "newsletters" to awaken a dormant contact who sets off another 10 × 10 × 10 chain reaction.

Like any skill, networking takes time and practice, but eventually it can become as regular as breathing.

Master Hui and his disciples had burned all the new fuel, even though the icy wind had not yet subsided. "Do not worry," said Shen Ti. "More fuel will arrive in the morning."

Master Hui chuckled. "You have become a magician, Shen Ti?"

"Not at all. The widow's son was so happy with my archery lessons that his mother praised my teaching to all her friends. Three young boys will be here soon for hunting lessons."

A man with many hats. "Which hat shall I wear today?" Marc Bender (Newton, MA), writer, producer, and media consultant, asks himself every morning. Bender has made a career out of communicating ideas for political candidates, corporations, non-profit groups, and government agencies. Interestingly, Bender has never spent a cent to attract clients. All his work comes through a vast personal network he's constructed over the past decade.

In college and graduate school, where his interests lay in

history and international relations, Bender initially donated his services to various local and national political campaigns. "It was an obvious decision," he recalls. "Since I was then an unproven commodity, only someone in the depths of despair would welcome me aboard. And there's nothing more desperate than a politician on the ropes."

The resulting network of contacts funneled work to the political consulting firm he formed several years after receiving his master's degree. After working on a variety of gubernatorial, congressional, and senatorial races, Bender began selling his "proven" communication skills to corporations and executives who'd suffered from negative newspaper coverage: "I would read *The New York Times* and clip articles about people and businesses getting bad press because they weren't communicating very well. I'd write to them, explaining how I could solve their problems. For every ten letters, I would get four interviews. At the end of each interview, I would refuse to leave until I'd gotten at least three more names of potential clients. My pool of contacts and referrals kept growing until I had a steady stream of work flowing in the door."

Since then, Bender has used his networking expertise to turn almost any experience into cold cash. Recently he took four months off to participate in a mountain-climbing expedition on the Sino-Soviet border. As soon as he returned, he revived his network and, sure enough, found a TV producer who needed help with a new documentary series on China. Says Bender, "As an entrepreneur, I've found ways to make nearly anything I do in life applicable to some project or other. I just plug it into the right network and watch it take off."

THE THIRD RING: PUTTING YOUR MAILMAN TO WORK

Whether you realize it or not, you're already a student of direct-mail advertising; every day you undoubtedly find your mailbox stuffed with "junk mail." From now on, look at those flyers, brochures, and solicitations carefully before you heave them into the trash bin. When you understand it better, you'll know that direct mail can put a powerful (and nonoffensive) money-making tool into your marketing mix.

Direct mail works for everything from newsletters to books, from software to hardware, and from dog walking to garden rototilling services. It reaches large numbers of people and also allows you to constantly refine your own more selective lists of prospects. To save money, you can start off using a small number of names from several different mailing lists, testing each to see how many responses you get. Lists that perform well in the test will also do well when used in full. You can always throw in samplings from other lists to test how they perform, thus experimenting with new audiences for your product.

Consider the case of newsletter publisher Robert J. George who, after finishing a tour of duty with the Marines in 1970, raised enough capital to launch three newsletters: *Aviation Monthly*, which condensed FAA reports of light aircraft accidents (morbid, but extremely useful to pilots); *Real Estate Investing*, which printed how-to information on managing commercial real estate; and *Business Monthly*, which offered basic management and financial advice to small business owners. George concentrated his marketing efforts on direct mail, and built his publications up to circulation levels of more than 25,000 each. By the mid-seventies his company, United Media, had sales of $6 million and published 12 newsletters, all built up through direct mail. In 1976 George sold United Media to Harcourt Brace and Jovanovich, and became a vice president of the company. By 1979 he was ready to start a new venture, and launched Boston Publishing Company, which most recently co-published the very successful book series titled *The Vietnam Experience*, which has sold more than three million copies. George recommends that knowing your audience is the key to successful direct-mail marketing. "Everything that worked best for me," he says, "worked because I could identify with the audience. I knew their needs, found a special niche, then filled it. If you have that closeness with your target audience, you've got your best chance for success."

When Barbara Brabec began publishing the *National Home Business Report*, she allowed her direct-mail effort to grow along with her business. "I started with mailings of two hundred, then five hundred, then one thousand, and so on. I can now afford to put ten thousand brochures into the mail at once, and can predict exactly what kind of response I'm going to get because I've kept such careful records of the response to every mailing I've

made in the past. The money generated from each mailing has
always enabled me to get to the next level."

While many have made their fortunes in direct mail, a far
greater number have lost their shirts. Direct-mail advertising is a
tricky science, and one false move can wipe out your whole marketing budget. Testing a variety of lists will give you a lot of information, but the information may be that *none* of them will make
you any money. The *choice* of lists, the *content* of what you mail,
and the *timing* of the mailing all dictate the outcome. Entrepreneurs who have no prior experience with direct mail should carefully study one of the marketing bibles listed in the SE Library
(Section III) before putting their life savings on the line. They
should also collect and analyze a wide variety of direct-mail
pieces and consider the following pointers:

1. *Be realistic about your response.* What would you consider an acceptable response rate for a promotional mailing targeted at businesses? Twenty-five percent? Thirty percent? Ten
percent? Try *one* percent. That's right—if you mail out 10,000
promotional pieces using a commercial mailing list and get back
100 responses, you should be pleased. You might do better—say,
two to three percent—if you were mailing to a consumer audience, but never count on more than one to two percent when you
project your cash flow.

Can you make money on such low returns? The answer depends on the price of your product. If you figure that a mailing
will cost you $275 per thousand solicitations on the average,
10,000 pieces will cost you $2,750. If you get 100 responses and
your product sells for $20, or a total of $2,000, you'll soon be
broke. But if your product goes for $250, your income from the
mailing would be $25,000, or a profit of $22,500. Now, that's
profit!

This simple arithmetic should teach you the value of aggressive pricing. If your market resists high prices, you'll want to
think twice about taking the direct-mail route. The most important rule of direct mail? Never count on a miracle.

Tom Kasner learned this lesson the hard way, and was lucky
enough to survive for another round of marketing. When health
issues surrounding microwave radiation began surfacing in the
mid-seventies, Kasner saw the need for a health publication that

would summarize important facts. Since he had no direct-mail experience, he unrealistically planned on a ten-percent response. Fortunately for him, the price of the newsletter was high enough to sustain his one-half-percent response until he scrounged up the cash to do another mailing, this time approaching it with more realistic expectations.

2. *Never skimp on packaging.* Obviously, you can increase the profitability of a mailing campaign by lowering its cost. Since you can't reduce postage costs (at the time of this writing, $111 per thousand for bulk mail), you could cut the quantity or quality of the pieces themselves, perhaps just sending a one-page flyer with an order form at the bottom. Beware, though, because such shortcuts inevitably spell direct-mail suicide. The wizards of direct mail long ago concluded that promo packages with four-to-six-page letters, repetitive brochures, and various other "inserts" get significantly better percentage returns than skimpy packages. Buyers like to be wooed, and feel insulted when they aren't. And shoddy mailings deliver the unkindest cut of all.

Let's say you can afford a letter, a brochure, and an order card. Is that enough? Not quite: no matter how much you have to economize, never send out a mailing without a business reply envelope. It costs you more to retrieve the mail, but numerous studies have proved that the easier you make it for potential buyers to respond, the better the chances they will respond.

Similarly, spring for an 800 toll-free number if you can afford it, and get a MasterCard/Visa agreement from a commercial bank. An 800 number can double or triple your response, and getting money via credit cards is as good as cash in hand (the bank charges you a small percentage on each order, but it's usually well worth it). Since many answering services will cover 800 numbers, you don't have to actually buy a toll-free line yourself. You just pay a monthly answering-service fee.

Again, research your own mailbox. Study lots of promo packages to see how other people handle letters, brochures, envelopes, and order cards. Much of your junk mail has been designed by marketing professionals and represents years of collective experience. Never feel shy about borrowing a pro's good ideas. As SE Charles Levin points out: "Because ideas can't be copyrighted you might as well use those that work. If you see an effective promotional package or design approach that attracts your attention, take it. Why not get the benefit from the thousands of dollars that someone else probably paid to get the concept developed? No one will get upset at seeing your product in someone else's garb."

3. *Know thy mailing lists.* One of the interesting phenomena of the Techno Age is that computers compile mailing lists day and night. Just call up any list broker—they're in the Yellow Pages under "advertising: direct mail"—to discover the tens of thousands of mailing lists anyone can rent. You can also find a variety of lists in a massive directory published by Standard Rate and Data Service (see SE Library, Section III), which breaks down available lists into common categories (e.g., medical, real estate) and profiles the people on them.

No matter how enticing you find such descriptions, however, determine the original source of the names, how recently the addresses have been updated, and what buying habits the people on the list display. If, say, you were looking for a good list of computer stores, you would avoid one compiled from telephone books because that list would include TV, radio, and game stores that happen to carry a $50 personal computer or two. Instead, you'd prefer a list of bona fide computer outlets known to carry name-brand items.

Similarly, if you were marketing a new kind of exercise machine that sells for $300, you'd want a list of people with a history of purchasing health and exercise equipment in that price range, not merely a list of health- and fitness-conscious people who may only buy vitamins, running shoes, or jump ropes. In any case, no matter how well you conceive and execute your promo package, you won't attract customers from an unqualified audience.

Obviously, the most qualified list for your product will always come from your own past customers. If you're running a retail operation, you can always get names and addresses as a routine part of writing up sales slips or by asking customers if they want to be on your mailing list. The resulting list will be ideal for selling a new product or service you're adding to your repertoire. Your mailings won't be as large as those sent to purchased lists, but your response will be considerably better. Just remember, though, that all of the above rules still apply: even if all the people on your list have bought your product in the past, you'll still get more takers if you treat them as cold prospects.

One company, Editorial Experts, Inc., markets extensively through self-compiled lists. Editorial Experts distributes books for professional writers and editors, holds seminars on various aspects of publishing, and publishes an informative newsletter called *The Editorial Eye*. Anytime someone subscribes to the newsletter or purchases a book, the name goes onto a mailing list for the seminar promotions. Seminar attendees are likewise placed on mailing lists for the book promotions. "We've been doing that for the past seven years," says Mara Adams, the company's vice-president. "The technique works so well that we don't have to buy many commercial mailing lists."

4. *Time your mailings exquisitely.* Unfortunately, there is some disagreement among the experts about the ideal time to conduct direct-mail campaigns. Traditional wisdom says to avoid the summer months because many people are on vacation then. (This seems reasonable, although some experts claim that you can still get good results in the summer if you're mailing to businesses.) Many direct-mail professionals also regard April as a bad time to sell through the mail, because at that time both individuals and companies are scrambling to pay their taxes.

The one time that *everyone* agrees to avoid is mid-November through December, because bulk mail can be delayed as much as five to six weeks or lost altogether during the holiday season. (At other times it's only slightly slower than first-class mail, but when things get tight in the post office, bulk mail goes straight to the bottom of the priority list.) What if your product would make a perfect Christmas gift? Do your mailing in October.

Shen Ti entered the house shaking his head. "I will not be replenishing our wood supply today," he confessed to Master Hui.

"The young men did not wish to learn the art of hunting?" inquired the Master.

Shen Ti shook his head. "No. They already know how to hunt. The widow delivered the wrong message, praising the quality of my bow and arrows, for which the young men came to trade. Now I must make a bow a day, if we are to have the fuel we need."

Striving for a long-lived success. When Richard Golob (Cambridge, MA) joined the staff of the Smithsonian Institution's Center for Short-Lived Phenomena in 1975, he dreamed about one day turning the government operation into an independent nonprofit organization from which he could profit in terms of steady employment at work he loved. The Center gathered and disseminated unique information on events such as earthquakes, volcanoes, and comets, and Golob assumed that an audience of science buffs would eagerly buy the Center's information. Several years later Golob did take over the Center, but selling its information turned out to be considerably harder than he had imagined.

After struggling for several years to keep the Center from becoming a short-lived phenomenon itself, Golob began brainstorming about newsletters and other publications that would be based on information exclusive to his organization's data banks. The result was the *Oil Spill Intelligence Report (OSIR)*, a weekly newsletter that reports exclusive information about oil spills occurring anywhere in the world. With the backing of Cahners Publishing Company, the oil-pollution newsletter began spreading and soon piped in enough cash to help offset the Center's operating costs. With the Center on its way to stability, Golob formed a new outfit, World Information Systems, which published yet another environmental newsletter, the *Hazardous Materials Intelligence Report (HMIR)*.

Both newsletters carry hefty subscription fees (*OSIR* sells for $397 per year in the U.S., *HMIR* for $325) and generally attract subscribers who work for corporations, government agencies, and research institutions. Since Golob has targeted such a specific market, he's had to build up his subscription base through carefully planned and researched mailings. Explains Golob, "We rarely buy mailing lists from a commercial list broker. Instead we get them from companies that sponsor environmental regulation conferences, or companies that sell a specific product for managing oil spills or hazardous waste. We also go to the government and use the Freedom of Information Act to get lists of companies that are responsible for pollution problems."

Golob stresses the importance of creatively packaging direct-mail material. "The hardest part of making a sale through the mail is to get your information onto people's desks when they're being bombarded by a million other selling pitches. That's why the envelope for *HMIR* mailings was designed to look like an urgent correspondence from the Environmental Protection Agency. People get a little nervous, and they open it. It's somewhat of a scare tactic, but it works."

Golob warns, however, that after the sale, a product must ultimately sell itself: "You can't confuse, insult, frustrate, or disappoint your readers. Try your hardest to make sure that their encounter with your publication is a positive one and that at least once during the year they learn something worth more to them than the subscription rate. If you don't have staying power, then direct mail isn't worth a damn." With a 70 to 80 percent renewal rate, Golob's publications have the staying power he strives to achieve.

THE FOURTH RING: SPREADING THE WORD
TO THE MASSES

For many people new to the business world, marketing means advertising. If you want to sell a product or service, you run an ad in the appropriate place, then sit back and wait for the cash register to ring. Not quite: advertising can drain a marketing budget dry, and SE's usually ransack every conceivable free opportunity before coughing up hard cash for media space. Furthermore, if direct mail is a tricky science, advertising makes it look like child's play. To appreciate the high cost of advertising, consider how much *one* full-page ad costs in *The Wall Street Journal* (all editions): $75,000! Some national magazines charge $15,000, $20,000, and more for a single page. Individual TV and radio spots can run many thousands of dollars—often for production costs alone. Obviously, only well-funded enterprises can afford to play the big-time advertising game.

Does this mean that SE's shun all paid advertising? No. A distinctive ad in the Yellow Pages usually makes sense, as does spending a small sum for listings in national directories. Classified ads can also pay for themselves and generate a few bucks. Small ads in trade magazines might also be affordable and can give you important recognition. But unless you have an enormous start-up budget or can somehow slash media costs, you should probably put paid advertising toward the bottom of your list of marketing alternatives.

When SE's do buy paid advertising, they approach it, as usual, in a nontraditional fashion. That means negotiating and bartering your way into cheaper space or air time. In some trade magazines you can make an arrangement whereby the ad space doesn't cost you anything but you pay the magazine a percentage of resulting sales. For example, you might put an ad for a newsletter in a magazine, promising the publisher anywhere from thirty to fifty percent of the eventual revenues it generates. You risk merely the cost of designing, typesetting, and pasting up the ad. Richard Golob has successfully used this technique numerous times to promote his newsletters.

Another tactic for buying cheap space has been suggested by Jay Conrad Levinson in his excellent book *Guerrilla Marketing* (see SE Library, Section III). Levinson, a guerrilla marketer himself, recommends setting up a second business that calls itself an ad agency. This will entitle you to the fifteen-percent discount an ad agency usually receives. Generally what's needed is a separate checking account and some letterhead stationery. Levinson also suggests looking for cooperative advertising possibilities, in which manufacturers will actually pay *you* to mention their names or products in your ads. (Two sources for learning about co-op advertising opportunities are listed in Section III of the SE Library.)

If you do decide to buy space for a print, radio, or TV ad, you can save yourself some headaches by observing some important rules:

1. *Beware the "one-shot jackpot syndrome."* Never assume that one good ad in the right place will make you an instant winner. If you plow your entire marketing budget into one ad (not a difficult feat, considering the high cost of national ad space) and

wait for the checks to start sailing in, you'll get quite a shock when the only envelopes piling up in your mailbox are bills.

The one-shot jackpot syndrome often afflicts technical firms such as computer and software companies that can't wait to grab a share of the market. Since a full-color ad in a major computer magazine runs anywhere from $5,000 to $10,000 for a one-time pop, and the costs of producing the ad can run anywhere from $2,000 to $5,000, you must recoup $7,000 to $15,000 in revenue just to break even. And that can be tough.

The following rule usually applies: *only repeated advertising works*. Moreover, an ad often needs to appear regularly in more than one place for people to take notice of your product and reach for their wallets. The rule holds true especially for television and radio advertising. Whereas a print ad remains in a newspaper or magazine until someone throws it out, a TV or radio spot flashes across the tube, then wings its way to Alpha Centauri. Out of sight, out of mind. If you can't afford a *sustained* advertising campaign, fall back on free media, grass-roots selling, and direct mail.

A year before the personal-computer craze fully hit, three techno whizzes developed a new product that would boost the power of personal computers. Despite objections from their marketing consultant, they socked all their remaining capital into a full-page, full-color ad in the most expensive computer magazine they could find. All they had to sell was twenty of the boards to break even, and thirty to make it worthwhile, they figured. The trio even counted on an original-equipment manufacturer ordering by the thousands. As it turned out, they would have been grateful to sell two. Or one.

Disheartened and broke, the three SE's were forced to work for someone else while they saved more cash. On the next round they tried a combination of limited direct mail, free media, and six small ads in modest publications. By the fourth ad they began to see some results, and by the sixth they captured the kind of manufacturer interest they needed to make it big.

2. *Stay away from image advertising.* AT&T, IBM, and Mobil can comfortably spend megabucks enhancing their images rather than touting their products. Most SE's, though, can't afford to project a handsome image at the expense of selling their wares. Keep your focus on your product or your service's stellar virtues.

One would-be computer entrepreneur began selling his software consulting service through a small ad in several regional business magazines. His initial ad was pitched at creating an elite image of his service—the Rolls-Royce of RAMs and ROMs. Unfortunately, no one ever learned what his firm actually did. And in a market that's becoming more competitive every day, few people will bother to find out. Two generations of ads later, he learned to give potential customers good reason to call his firm. The lesson? Image never comes before content.

3. *Sink your hook.* Good advertising pulls people to your shore. Because it makes your product or service seem indispensable, it prompts action. To capture your audience's imagination, try to force your potential customers to analyze an aspect of their lives they may have previously ignored: "Wow! I *am* wasting time or money or working less efficiently than I could." Or, "Gosh, I can't live another day without that gizmo."

Another kind of hook piques the reader's curiosity so that he or she will at least read on. While curiosity may kill the cat, it certainly lures the customer. One widely circulated promotional from a business service once used the following hook: "Throw this out and do your competitor a favor." Who wouldn't spend at least a moment finding out what the service has to offer? Beware, though: don't use teasers that ask a question to which the viewer can say "No" and stop reading, such as "Are you wasting . . . ?" The same goes for conditions like "If you are wasting . . ." Assume that people who see your ad are already looking for reasons *not* to read it; never offer them an easy one.

4. *Get down to basics.* An ad isn't worth a subway token unless it clearly shows people your product's benefits. After you've set your hook, don't waste time trying to entertain. Focus on benefits, not features, and describe them in terms of the Project Themes discussed in Chapter 4.

Let's say you own a specialty fitness shop, and you want to run an ad or a radio or TV spot. After intriguing people with your free customized training program, done by computer, you explain exactly what your store has to offer customers: savings in money, savings in time (one-stop shopping for all fitness needs), improved health, and a potentially longer life.

5. *Hold your head above the crowd.* Assuming you've sparked people's interest and have explained your product, you must distinguish yourself from your competition. There's no need

to knock the competition over its head, but you can imply that your product or service outshines all others.

In the case of the fitness store, you might say: "The only store with a full-time consultant who holds a Ph.D. in sports training" . . . or offer: "No other store includes a monthly training newsletter free to every customer," or, "The only fitness store that gives you computer power." Whatever you do, give people the impression that you're not just one of many options, but the *only* choice.

As with direct mail, study existing advertising. Analyze TV, radio, and print ads for their strong and weak points. Try to determine why the ads evoke particular responses, then try redesigning weak ones. Borrow features that seem to work.

As the days grew steadily warmer, Master Hui interrupted the busy bow maker. "Shen Ti, you have made enough bows to arm the entire state, but we no longer need fuel."

Shen Ti finished wrapping the grip on a sturdy bow. "Perhaps not, but I have circulated news of my bow-making ability, and I am now besieged with orders. If I work all spring, we will have more than enough fuel for the next winter."

Roughing it in high style. Thomas Barquinero, a twenty-seven-year-old account executive with a big New York advertising agency, leads a dual life. By day he manages the Toyota account in Saudi Arabia; by night and on weekends he pitches tents, shells shrimp, makes beds, and pours drinks at his Inn in the Wilderness, the world's first "sophisticated camping resort."

Barquinero had always fantasized about managing a country inn when he retired, but like a true SE, he made his fantasy come true a few decades before he turned sixty-five. On a business trip to the Virgin Islands, Barquinero stayed overnight at an offbeat hotel that consisted of a series of tents pitched on the beach but with full-size beds inside. Intrigued by the concept, Barquinero returned to New York with an idea: camping in style.

Located in the scenic Berkshire Mountains of western Massachusetts, Barquinero's inn includes king-size tents equipped with Japanese futons, clean sheets, rugs, and rattan tables. A raw bar sits outside the tents, and the strains of Vivaldi and Beethoven waft through speakers hung in the trees. Guests dine on elegant food, sipping fine wine by outdoor fires where even the mosquitoes wear tuxedos. For such sumptuous surroundings guests gladly pay a fee of $275 per couple, which includes tickets to nearby Tanglewood, a renowned outdoor concert center. "People love the great outdoors," Barquinero explains, "but they associate camping with a lot of little kids running around, and Winnebegos blocking the view. This is camping without the hassles."

To advertise his venture, Barquinero used every marketing trick in the book: "I spent long hours after work, banging out personal letters to old friends. That's how I finally got the site—a buddy let me use his land for free. I also wrote all the copy for the brochure. I wrote it, and rewrote it, and showed it to everybody. I spent entire weekends standing in front of Lincoln Center handing out flyers."

"Targeting your audience is very tricky," he advises. "You have to know exactly who you're going after. The headline on my first flier said, 'Introducing Luxury Camping for Urban Dilettanti.' It was too highbrow. I didn't think it would be, but it was. It didn't go over well at all."

After evaluating his progress, Barquinero decided to try some paid advertising. Since he wanted to attract young urban professionals, he placed ads in the *Village Voice* and *New York* magazine. He also wrote a radio commercial to entice affluent couples to his resort. Taking advantage of the Tanglewood feature, he slotted a commercial on a classical music station. As a result of his small-scale but highly focused media campaign, he soon sold out every weekend for the entire summer.

Barquinero has extensive plans for future enhancements and a new version of his original idea. Whatever path he chooses he's sure to apply the proven maxim that creativity, more than dollars, spells success in advertising.

EXERCISE 6: PUT ON YOUR MARKETING HAT

1. If you have any inhibitions about promoting yourself, it's time to put them away. Write a press release about something special you did this week. Or write one for an SE enterprise that you've thought about starting. Imagine that you're trying to get *The Wall Street Journal* to write an article about you or your project. Before picking up your pen or touching your keyboard, review the elements of a good press release. Remember, the idea of a press release is to do all the work for the reporter: it should be brief but still answer the whos, whats, whens, wheres, and whys.

2. Imagine that you've been hired as the P.R. director for a company that manufactures a revolutionary new kind of indestructible, inflatable life raft. Your job depends on the raft making a big debut splash. What kinds of P.R. stunts can you think of that would be sure to attract the press (like demonstrating one in a Beverly Hills swimming pool filled with sharks or alligators)? After writing down a few, use the same kind of thinking for a project of your own design.

7
ONWARD AND UPWARD: MANAGING YOUR SUCCESS

To the ecstasy of everyone, warm spring winds finally bathed the region, and Master Hui celebrated the long-awaited change in season by gathering his disciples in his garden to deliver his most important lecture.

"How does a garden grow?" the Master asked with a twinkle in his eye. "The way all life forms grow, with ch'i. Ch'i, or cosmic energy, flows everywhere, and takes on different forms in different seasons. Now, in spring, ch'i dances with life, enabling the plant life to again flourish. Look at the first green sprouts in my garden; what do they teach us about ch'i?"

After staring intently at the garden, Shen Ti answered, "Events in the cosmos occur according to their nature. If the farmer tries to hasten his crop's growth by pulling on the stalks he will thwart their nature and kill the very source of his nourishment."

BRINGING HOME THE LETTUCE

Ever since our ancestors stopped stalking dinner with a club and began raising it with a hoe, we've had gardening in our blood. No matter how far from the farm we may live, we all retain some intuition about the *ch'i* that makes things grow. SE's rely heavily on such instinct, because every project has a life form

171

of its own, requiring thorough planning and preparation, diligent care and nurturing, protection from pests, patient pruning, and careful harvesting. And like a good gardener, every SE knows how to allow each unique project to grow at its own pace, expending its own natural flow of energy.

Earlier in this book you learned how to identify and plant the seeds of a good idea by applying the test of Universal Project Themes, and designing a sound marketing campaign. Now you can turn your attention toward maintaining the best possible conditions for your seedling to prosper and produce a harvestable crop. In this chapter you'll find out about five important phases through which every project passes before it grows to full fruition. As you read on, you'll discover ways to balance your enterprise and the life-style it will allow you to have.

As Shen Ti observed, you can't make your corn grow by pulling on it. Likewise, successful management requires patience. As an SE, you must learn to adjust your expectations to the realities of the marketplace, never counting on an overnight smash hit—such success is usually a fluke and seldom lasts long. Most perenially stable businesses take two or three years to reach the "steady harvest" state. So during the tumultuous start-up phase, try to enjoy the ups and learn from the downs. And if you ever think about throwing in the towel, just remember this maxim: Everything in the cosmos happens in its own time.

Phase 1: Watching How Your Garden Grows

If you've properly planned and planted your garden, you'll soon see some healthy sprouts popping up through the ground. But unless you keep a vigilant eye on the crop and give it what it needs to grow, you could still see your effort fail. An SE project requires constant monitoring and nurturing. In fact, without such care the hottest idea can wither and die. To maintain momentum, SE's practice the following "green-thumb" rules:

1. *Keep track of your project.* What you don't know about your project *will* hurt you. Many businesses—even prestigious corporate giants—bite the dust because people at the top have no idea of what's really going on below. When the country's twelfth largest bank went down the tubes in 1984 and had to be bailed out by the government, the top executives themselves admitted

they had no idea how bad things really were. So whether you're a one-woman lemonade stand or a hundred-person fashion-design studio, your survival depends on awareness.

One kind of monitoring involves paying keen attention to numbers. Don't just keep monthly financial records, *study* them. How much money will you realistically bring in over the next three months? How much will you have to pay out in overhead and other costs? Are you headed for a cash crunch two months from now? Ask yourself such questions every week. If you don't know the answers, get them.

Another type of monitoring entails deep reflection. Does this project seem to be going where you want it to go? Have your initial assumptions proven correct? Has your marketing hit the bull's-eye? Does your enterprise give you opportunities to employ your creativity? Does it enable you to live how and where you want? Does it afford you the kind of life-style you're seeking, or does it jeopardize it? Does it allow you to maintain the values you uphold as important?

The last two points are extremely important, for as SE Dwight Platt discovered when his business boomed and his marriage simultaneously evaporated, it's easy to lose sight of what really has meaning for you. Money can be a trap, and it takes constant assessment and reassessment to ensure that you're not getting into something that will force you to make wrenching decisions at a later date.

Many SE's record their reflections in a business diary or journal. Käthe Ăna, an oral historian and storyteller, recommends keeping three kinds of journals: a professional journal, a personal journal, and an ideas journal. "I look at each one depending on what I need," she says. "I look at my professional journal to see what I've accomplished, and my personal journal to see how I've grown. And if I begin to wonder how I came to be doing what I'm doing, I just pick up my ideas journal and look at the course I've been charting. My ideas journal also reminds me of everything I'd like to do in the future, so I never lose track of where I'd like to be heading."

2. *Control your growth.* In the business world, as in the plant kingdom, faster growth does not necessarily mean better growth. In fact, too much growth can topple even the tallest tree. When a business grows too fast it becomes impossible to monitor,

and dumb things begin to happen, like an executive waking up one morning to find out that the company owes far more money than it has in the bank and the accounts-receivable file.

This kind of scenario quite frequently befalls young high-tech companies that strike it big, the classic case being the Osborne Computer Company. Osborne Computer experienced "hypergrowth" from a $900,000 investment to $100 million in annual sales in less than two years, then soon found itself in dire straits. The reason? In the process of hyperexpansion management let go of the financial controls and no one knew the magnitude of the cash-flow problem until it was too late. The moral is: Never let the growth of an enterprise exceed your ability to control and monitor it. Once you've lost control, you may never get it back.

3. *Allow your project to grow where it naturally thrives.* SE's often discover that what they originally set out to do works, but quite often in surprising ways. In such cases it's often best to continue with the project, momentarily letting it take you where it will. Chocolate sculptor photo creator Victor Syrmis, for example, found that his idea caught on, but not as he'd expected. "My original concept was to make chocolate reproductions of portraits. I thought we'd do whole faces. Now we're getting automated and are doing gift boxes that have faces in twenty little pieces. We're also buried in orders for chocolate reproductions of everything from company logos to pictures of nudes, gearshifts, trees, and cows. The main thing I learned from this was the need to be flexible and meet the changing demands of the business."

Every successful SE will offer valuable tips about nurturing a project, but it all boils down to the fine art of keeping a dual gaze on today's problems and tomorrow's prospects.

Master Hui asked, "Do you know why the good farmer needs no almanac or calendar?"

Shen Ti replied, "He knows that his own ch'i and the ch'i of his crops draw from the same source. His ch'i tells him when to plant, when to prune, and when to harvest. In that way, the good farmer is never taken by surprise."

The case of the shifting client base. Both Marilyn Dashe and Jean Thomson (Minneapolis, MN) were in their thirties when they entered the master's program in English at the University of Minnesota. Dashe had spent five years in a paramedical career, which she found too limiting, while Thomson had been teaching eighth-grade English, an equally limiting job.

By the end of the master's program, however, both women had decided that although they enjoyed writing and teaching English, they wanted more from life than grading themes and discussing water imagery in Melville. When their professors at the university agreed that college jobs would be hard to land anyway, the two women decided that if colleges would not pay them to teach and write, perhaps someone else would. Armed with nothing but their credentials, some teaching experience, and a lot of guts, Dashe and Thomson approached the university extension about teaching business-writing seminars to nonacademics. The extension division accepted their scheme, and before long corporate employees were crowding their classrooms.

Using the seminars as a starting point for higher ambitions, Dashe and Thomson kept lists of all their students, thereby identifying companies likely to want or need writing seminars. They would then phone the companies to sell an in-house business-writing workshop. Closing such sales took time and effort, but eventually paid off. After refining their techniques, Dashe and Thomson decided to investigate the computer world. Since Dashe had worked briefly as a technical writer at a computer company, she renewed her contacts there and soon landed a large contract to write a computer manual. Knowing very little about computers and documentation, the two entrepreneurs played a good Techno Age hand, drawing on their English skills, learning computerese along the way. The manual took them a grueling six months to finish, but the results pleased both them and their client. Dashe says, "We found that the most pressing need for writing and teaching was in computers—and that our market should be focused, not toward the regular business people, but toward computers. We also found that we really had the skills necessary for mastering a technical field, and that all we had to do was work harder to fill a gap."

By gently shifting the focus of their enterprise from general business to the computer industry, Dashe and Thomson have built a rapidly expanding business. While they still teach at the university, their company, Dashe & Thomson, Inc., now owns four computers and employs fourteen technical writers. Jean Thomson attributes their success in part to their forward-looking, flexible attitude: "It's important to steer the ship with one hand, but always to keep the other hand shading your eyes, looking toward the horizon. I think we do that."

Phase 2: Maintaining Your Garden

Once your garden begins to grow, you must keep it free of weeds, prune dead growth, and thin out overgrown areas that tax the available nutrients and offer a feast for pests. An SE must also constantly clean the shop to keep from getting into unnecessary hassles with suppliers, creditors, and investors, and from being devoured by predators such as the IRS. The following rules will help you keep your garden clean:

1. *Maintain an exemplary credit slate.* The best thing you can do for your fledgling enterprise is to plan your cash flow so you can pay *all* your bills on time. A solid credit history can save your life in the future. Not only will it put you in a better bargaining position with your current and future suppliers, but if you should need a cash injection from a bank, you'll look like a good bet for a loan. To look good, stay clean.

Dal La Magna, aka Tweezerman, agrees: "The success of my business and my business strategy comes down to one thing: keeping current with all my bills and building my credit line with every possible opportunity. I don't pay a day early and I don't pay a day late. I don't play with float [writing rubber checks on the assumption that other checks won't be cashed for a while], so I never risk bouncing checks. To beef up my credit and get through cash crunches I take out small loans or use one of my ten credit cards. The main thing is, I pay them off on time. That makes me a model citizen."

2. *Keep an open channel with those to whom you owe*

money. What if you do get yourself into a jam and can't pay your creditors, the bank, or meet a projection for an investor? Does that immediately condemn you to a future without credit? Only if you hide. The solution, as Bob Kuzara recommends, is an open line of communication. "If you're having problems, the worst thing you can do is avoid a supplier. Call up the people you owe money to and explain your situation, and propose a payment plan. As long as people know that a steady dribble of money will be coming in, they'll leave you alone. There might be some hard feelings in the beginning when you tell a supplier that the invoice due in sixty days will be spread out over six months. But when the six months is up and the bill is paid, you're still in business. You might have to pay cash with that supplier next time around, but you'll probably be in a better position to do so. Then you can work on reestablishing an extension of credit. I have plenty of suppliers who had to wait a year or more to get paid. But I'm still doing business with them and my credit record is just fine. The bottom line is, keep the dribble going and you won't burn any bridges."

3. *Keep a good clean set of books.* Once a good accountant has set up your books, your job is to maintain scrupulous monthly records. Such diligence will give you the basic information you need to keep your enterprise running and also keep you out of trouble at the end of the year.

When it does come time for the annual tallying, take every legitimate tax deduction you or your accountant can find. Don't wave red flags by claiming enormous amounts for travel and entertainment or by trying to write off 98 percent of your monthly house rent or mortgage payments as office space. The immediate cash benefit from distorting what you owe and the momentary thrill of beating the system may well cost you penalties down the line. When in doubt, use the SE rule that no tax maneuver is worth the effort if you think you'll lose even a wink of sleep over it.

Marc Bender, who survived an audit several years ago, offers this advice: "Play by the rules. You don't have to be devious, and you don't have to strain the imagination to get a fair deal out of your tax situation. I went into the audit girding my loins, steeling myself for an IRS 'search-and-destroy' mission. To my surprise I was not asked any unreasonable questions. And since my conscience was clear, I was pretty casual during the whole process.

Ultimately, I think it was my relaxed demeanor that made the experience painless."

Phase 3: Harvesting Your Crops

There are times to sow and times to reap. As we saw in Chapter 4, you must properly time the sowing of a new project. Similarly, you must know just when to commence the reaping of profits. Your harvesting decisions depend equally on both financial and life-style goals. You must always balance the money machine that puts soup on your table against your longer-term personal needs. Skip Kates, a senior at Babson College, and founder of Kandy Man, a chocolate novelty company, has wrestled with the balance: "There are two ways to operate a business. One is for the future, the other is for your pocket. Anytime you make a sale, you can put the money in your pocket. The other way is to put the money into your business and keep building it up. If you play your cards right, the future rewards will be well worth the wait."

Most SE's take the long-range view, both because they have faith in their efforts and because they don't need instant gratification. The founders of Ashton Tate, the superstar software company, for example, took minimal salaries their first two years even though the company grossed $20 million. Why the low take when they could have written paychecks and bonuses for whatever amount they wanted? Doing so would have run counter to their bootstrap philosophy, which entailed stretching every dollar and allowing the company to become as strong as possible in terms of development and marketing. That kind of thinking paid off; by the fourth year, the company's annual sales blossomed to a whopping $40 million.

"How does the wise farmer harvest his crops?" asked Master Hui.

"In two ways," replied Shen Ti. "He harvests a winter's supply of food and the next spring's supply of seeds."

Kitchen-table chemistry. Marion Landis (Cleveland, OH) could hardly see through her dirty kitchen windows, but no matter how hard she scrubbed or what commercial product she used, she couldn't make them sparkle. Frustrated, Landis decided she'd develop her own heavy-duty cleaner to get the job done. One spring morning in 1978, she sat down at her kitchen table with a telephone, the Yellow Pages, and a Webster's unabridged dictionary. In an effort to get a crash course in cleaning chemistry, she called the research department at a local industrial chemical company and told a staff chemist she was in the process of developing a new glass cleaner, which had to be tough but nontoxic. Whenever the chemist threw an incomprehensible term at her, Landis quickly put the conversation on hold and looked it up in her dictionary. At the end of an hour, she had substantially added to her growing education and had arranged to receive free samples of potentially useful chemicals.

When the samples arrived, Landis used her newly acquired knowledge of cleaning chemistry to experiment with various combinations, whipping up all sorts of concoctions in her Mixmaster. For several weeks she labored in her makeshift kitchen laboratory, testing the results on heavily soiled pieces of glass she'd collected from a local wrecking company. Eventually she perfected Mr. Glass, a heavy-duty yet nontoxic glass cleaner. Satisfied that she had an effective and unique product, Landis decided to market it. "I knew that if I needed it, other people needed it too," she says. "And I really wanted to achieve something. I knew I had something valuable to contribute, and that if I just did my homework, I was qualified to speak out about it."

But how could she market and distribute Mr. Glass, given the fact that she hadn't raised any capital to start a business—all she had originally wanted to do was clean her kitchen windows. After more clever research, Landis contracted with an East Coast mail-order company. She says, "I decided on mail order for two reasons: the first was that I wouldn't have to pay for my own advertising, which was crucial since I didn't have any money. The second reason was that if I bombed, no one around here would ever know about it!"

When the mail-order company bought one hundred cases, a surprised Landis suddenly had to begin production, so she borrowed $1,500 from her husband and hired a packaging firm she found in the Yellow Pages. The first profits went to paying off her loan. After that, she wisely reinvested the money in product improvement, to make Mr. Glass more salable. She also succeeded in using free media to keep her marketing expenses down. Her campaign began with letters to the women's and new-product editors of major daily newspapers, who found her ideas and spunk newsworthy. The press coverage prompted invitations to appear on talk shows across the country, and even led to lucrative contracts with major department stores and national mail-order companies.

Mr. Glass is now distributed throughout the United States and Canada, with annual sales of more than 50,000 bottles, at between three and four dollars per bottle. Though Landis enjoys the income, she gets more of a thrill from having succeeded on nothing but ingenuity and a shoestring, against major odds. "In this world the rules are made by Procter and Gamble," she says triumphantly. "It's exhilarating to come up with a product of your own, a product that everybody wants." As her case shows, careful research, frugal spending, persistence—and the right chemistry—can lead to a clean balance sheet.

Phase 4: Rejuvenating Your Soil

Whether you work a twenty-square-foot vegetable garden or a two-thousand-acre field, you have to rotate your crops to keep the soil rich and supportive. Likewise, SE's always cultivate new ideas and variations on old themes to bring new chemistry and life to their businesses. New ideas or spin-offs greatly increase your options.

First, a spin-off idea may make more money than your original idea. You learn from doing, and each generation of ideas tends to capitalize on preceding ones. SE's know that spin-offs beget spin-offs, which beget spin-offs. Look at how Donald Itkin went from an academic-paper-editing service to a flashy advertising company. Or how Bobbi Wolf of Poemetrics went from delivering custom poems over the phone for three dollars to hand-calligraphy poems at twenty dollars apiece. Or how Richard Golob used his environmental newsletters to generate consulting assignments from his readers.

SE's also thrive on spin-offs because trends and the demands of the market continually change. The histories of small and large businesses alike testify to the value of flexibility and versatility. Changing national styles and tastes, or emerging technologies render old products obsolete and open markets for new ones. Look at how IBM was able to roll over from mechanical business machines into electric machines and then again into computers. That's flexibility on a grand scale!

On a smaller but no less impressive scale, Thomas Barquinero, founder of the popular Inn in the Wilderness, is now considering a variation on his successful project. It's called "luxury adventure travel" and includes a bike trip through the Green Mountains. "Campers" would go on a predetermined scenic bike ride, and when they arrived at their destination, their tents would be set up, along with a raw bar and a liquor bar. Eventually Barquinero plans to spin off into luxury hot-air-balloon rides through the French-vineyard countryside.

Finally, spin-offs keep you alert. Entrepreneurs need an ongoing surge of creativity to keep them alive, and spin-offs nicely satisfy that need. As Sanford Schwartzman suggests, "Half of success is keeping your mind flexed, by thinking about ways to improve your present business and ways to expand it into new areas. The entrepreneur's mind works best when it's living for today and tomorrow at the same time."

But while spin-offs can pyramid your ideas into ever-more-towering success, they can also threaten your stability if you don't observe certain rules:

1. *Time your spin-offs brilliantly.* A spin-off must hit an open window (Chapter 4), and it must also lie within range of your time, energy, and resources. Don't undertake a new venture, no matter how attractive or inspiring, if it will sap your strength and detract from your main preoccupation. Ill-timed spin-offs can put you out of business. As Richard Golob points out, "Entrepreneurs always run the risk of slipping into the 'I'm invincible' mode: they undertake all kinds of ancillary projects and drown in them. In our case we'd been collecting and cataloging information about science and technology, and it dawned on us that we ought to write a science almanac. So we prepared a book proposal, worked out a contract with a publisher, and

started on the book. To our dismay, for the next two years the project became an enormous sponge that soaked up every second of time and every cent it could find. The almanac is finally done. It's a great book, but it almost killed us!"

2. *Allow your spin-off to draw on existing resources.* A good spin-off project should require as little additional research and funding as possible, and it should draw on existing systems, customer bases, and other resources in new ways. Jonathan Pond, who is now president of Investment Management, Inc., also runs a small but growing publication called *Business Library Newsletter.* During his graduate-student days at the Harvard Business School, Pond did a lot of consulting and found that clients were constantly asking him to recommend good books on money management and other business topics. Since he was digging through stacks of books to get the information he needed for his consulting practice, he decided to start a publication that reviewed new books in the business field. To his surprise, no one in the business community seemed interested. Libraries, however, couldn't subscribe fast enough, and Pond has since created a specialty publication just for them.

Five years later, though Pond is primarily concerned with international investment strategies, he still uses SE techniques such as free media, conferences, and directory listings to promote his newsletter. "Every project has its own internal momentum," Pond says, "and although we're not marketing *Business Library Newsletter* aggressively, the subscriptions keep dribbling in and word gets around that we've got a good thing. It's a fine little project to work on the side."

3. *Spin-offs should stand on their own two feet.* While a good spin-off may draw on your existing resources, it must carry its own weight in terms of income and profits. Otherwise you may unwittingly allow it to drain rather than sustain your efforts. Treat every spin-off as a distinct profit center, never letting a strong project mask the weakness or unprofitability of another. Also, some projects do not differ enough from present ones to warrant spinning them off. As marketing consultant Jane Frank advises, "When you give people two hairline-close choices, you wind up confusing and aggravating them. You might even wind up putting them off and killing a sale."

"Tell us again of the parable of Lao Ching," requested Shen Ti.

The Master agreed. "Lao Ching grew the best persimmons in the province. The sweetest ones he ate himself, the inferior ones he sold at the market or stored for seeds. As time went by, Lao grew fatter and fatter, but the merchants eventually shunned his persimmons because the inferior seeds produced increasingly inferior trees and fruit. The moral, Shen Ti?"

"Give your best fruit to the buyer, but always save enough good seeds to protect the quality of your future crops."

Moving into the fast lane. An SE to the core, Stanley Plog has worn an odd assortment of hats throughout his life. Plog graduated *magna cum laude* from Occidental College, played first trombone with some major bands, and holds a Ph.D. in clinical psychology. To top it off, he founded Plog Research, Inc., a market-research company specializing in the travel and import auto industries. Not long ago he launched Showcase Rental Cars, an agency that rents fine imported cars—Peugeots, Saabs, Volvos, BMWs, and Alpha Romeos to business travelers and vacationers. Along with the luxury cars, Plog also offers luxury service: sparkling, well-maintained automobiles, immaculate rental offices, and friendly salespeople.

Showcase is actually a spin-off of Plog Research, whose market analysis showed that "a lot of people have unhappy traveling experiences. The fun part is what you do when you get there." Familiar with the auto and travel industries, and having spent his life giving marketing and positioning advice, Plog decided to redirect all that rich experience to a new market, making "getting there" half the fun. While Showcase naturally grew out of Plog Research, it also posed special marketing challenges.

"The object is to someday change the nature of the car-rental market," says Plog. "Right now we have to adapt to the big guys, Hertz and Avis. That's the fun part. If they sneeze, we catch a cold. But pretty soon that'll all change. We'll never be as big as Hertz or Avis, but our standards will be high enough to make them clean up their acts."

Plog estimates that he will open six to eight new Showcase offices each year for the next four years. Along with this ambitious expansion, Plog has also begun to create spin-offs from his spin-off, adding a limo rental to the import-auto-rental service. "We weren't planning on doing that for several years," says Plog, "but the opportunity came along sooner than we'd expected. We had to decide whether to jump the gun or wait until the projected time. Finally we figured that if the market's open now, we might as well get into it."

While Plog has become an expert at juggling resources among his various spin-offs and at hiring capable managers to keep his three-ring circus rolling, he admits that he's still "running like blazes," assuming disaster's around every corner. "But," he says assuredly, "that comes with the territory. Besides, it adds to the thrill!"

Phase 5: Planting Seeds for Your Future

The joy of cultivating a successful garden is partly annual, partly perennial. Once a crop has reached fruition, the gardener's mind drifts off to the next spring, dreaming of another planting and another harvest. Perhaps next time the gardener will go for a larger plot. Perhaps he or she will try some new crops or introduce a new technique or a new technology. Whatever the change, the dream never dies.

Once SE projects begin to bear fruit, their founders often shift their gaze toward the horizon as they begin to ask themselves, "What's next? Do I expand my present project into an empire? Do I follow a spin-off? Do I sell my business and seek a new challenge?"

In some cases, SE's sell their businesses outright and simply begin anew. In other cases, they modify their enterprises to make sure that they won't be forced into life-style and value compromises. Peter Barnes is a good example of the latter. After fourteen years of serving as a reporter for *Newsweek* and *The New Republic*, Barnes decided he'd spent enough time muckraking. "I'd flung my share of arrows at the big corporations, but inwardly feared they were invincible because no one else could deliver the goods we'd all grown so accustomed to having—the cars, stereos, bananas. I also concluded that I could never bring myself to hold a straight job. So why not create my own? Or better yet, the kind of enterprise I would like to work for?"

So as an intellectual exercise and a personal challenge, Barnes set out to start a nontraditional business that was compatible with his personal commitment to cooperative enterprise but which was also competitive in the marketplace. The answer was the Solar Center, which designs and installs solar heating systems in the San Francisco Bay Area. Started with five other partners, each of whom invested $5,000 and "worked hard but exuberantly for poverty-level wages," the Solar Center quickly grew into a thriving business, and Barnes found he could no longer make all his decisions by friendly conversation. He also found himself struggling with problems of growth: he needed to establish a hierarchical structure; he needed to pay some workers more than others; and he needed to form a board of directors. While Barnes made these concessions to growth, he never compromised his original vision of a cooperative venture. Under his new arrangement, some workers earn more money per year than others, but all employees nevertheless own equal shares of the company, and all owners have equal voting power. By looking for new ways to structure his company, Barnes and his co-workers found a way to make their company's growth and their personal goals work hand in hand.

Some SE's have found that merging with others is a good way to take care of growth problems. Look at how avant-garde Los Angeles publisher Jeremy Tarcher did it. Tarcher's career started in the mailroom of WNEW-TV in the mid-fifties, then took him through a winding course in the TV production and publishing fields. His initial publishing efforts in the early sixties focused on Hollywood personalities, but by the mid-seventies he had become strongly attracted to the personal-growth and transformation field. "I saw a small spark of consciousness," Tarcher says, "and began to see how many years I had been sleeping." His quest for personal enlightenment drove him to the leading edge of the human-growth movement, where he set his sights on publishing books that would help others use their full creative powers to transform their lives. His most popular book has been *Drawing on the Right Side of the Brain*.

To achieve what he wanted, though, Tarcher was faced with a dilemma: he didn't have the structure, capital, or experience to handle the kind of effort he had envisioned. Change course? Not Tarcher. Having built up his company from a $3,500 initial investment to billings of a million dollars a year, he wasn't about to give it up just because he ran out of capital. So he struck a deal with Houghton Mifflin whereby the old Boston publisher would provide sales, financial support, and an administrative structure, while Tarcher still controlled his own editorial show.

The arrangement worked for three years, during which time Tarcher's annual billings increased to $3 million. When Houghton Mifflin changed its own publishing vision, Tarcher returned to the lists of independent publishers. "I'm on my own again," he says, "but I've come up several rungs on the ladder. I've learned a great deal that will help me in the future." And what of the future? Tarcher sees himself in publishing for another five years while he develops other media for communicating the essence of personal transformation, such as videotapes, cassettes, and computer programs that interact with users. Whichever way the tide turns, Tarcher will find a way to passionately ride the current.

Other SE's, like Robert Schwartz, have skillfully pressed one success into another. Schwartz's various enterprises include a founding partnership in *New York* magazine, a Japanese hotel overlooking the Hudson, and a lavish conference center in an exquisite mansion in Tarrytown, New York. Today he directs the School for Entrepreneurs, which offers three-day workshops in which people learn how to unleash their entrepreneurial spirits. Still other SE's see the ongoing mission as taking their current project to the highest possible state of quality. For this breed of entrepreneur the project becomes a new Mount Everest to be reclimbed and reconquered every day. It becomes a reinvestment of time, energy, and money that marks the highest form of commitment.

"My Uncle Ming learned how to perfect cabbage farming," said Shen Ti.
"How so?" asked Master Hui.

"Uncle Ming had a cabbage farm but the rabbits devoured all his crops, so he started a rabbit farm. When the rabbits died of a mysterious disease, he buried them and raised worms. With the worms he caught fish, which he traded for more cabbage seeds, and with all the rabbits dead his cabbage farm has made him rich."

"Your point, Shen Ti?"

"No matter what Uncle Ming's business, it was the ch'i *of cabbage all along."*

A *steady course on the cutting edge*. "I went to school *not* to learn anything specific," recalls Geoffrey Rappaport (San Rafael, CA), referring to his decision to attend Monteith College. Monteith was an experimental school based on a great-books program that provided a solid liberal-arts education. After graduating, Rappaport worked in the Teacher Corps in Detroit, but as he became more politically active, he drifted on to San Francisco, where he lived in the Haight-Ashbury and worked painting signs.

Life in the Haight was "real education," according to Rappaport, but six months later he was invited to enroll in Berkeley's graduate school of arts and sciences as an undeclared graduate student. Says Rappaport, "I couldn't resist the opportunity and challenge. The school wanted to see how someone from a liberal-arts program like Monteith's would fare against students from more traditional programs. I wanted to see what I was worth in that environment, too." So Rappaport began studying the philosophy of education, and performed as well as anyone else. For the first few years he was content, and aspired to take on a university position when he finished with his doctorate. But by the fifth year he realized that academia was too fraught with petty politics, formalities, and unpleasant jockeying for position.

Rappaport took his master's degree, packed up his worldly possessions, left the university, and survived as a carpenter and an apprentice electrician. He also spent much of the next two years sitting in Tilden Park outside of Berkeley looking at clouds, trying to figure out what in life both made him happy and could support him. "I just dropped out of everything that everyone else had dropped into," Rappaport says, "and went into a state of deep inner reflection." During that period of meditation he realized that his real love in life came from being a craftsman. What surprised him, though, was the medium he chose: hair.

It all started when a friend jokingly suggested that he ought to go to beauty school. The more Rappaport thought about it, the more the idea appealed to him. It seemed like an honest trade, and he liked the idea of working in a licensed craft. It would also provide a steady income: "Like medicine, it's depression-proof," he says. "In fact, it's one of the few industries that can actually improve in worsening economic times. People always like to look better than their situations actually allow."

Musing led to action, and Rappaport soon enrolled in a one-year beauty-school program, where he met Frank Emmett, who would later become the most important teacher in Rappaport's life. "Frank taught me how to work creatively, how to think like a professional, and how to act like a professional." That knowledge served him well in his first job, which lasted only a few months because the salon that employed him went bankrupt. Packing his shears, he paid a visit to Emmett to discuss the state of the craft, and left as a fifty-percent partner in what was to become Supercuts, which evolved into one of the largest hair-cutting chains in the country.

"The planning took four to five hours," Rappaport recalls. "Frank said that we each had one half of a great idea. We decided that there were too few options: the expensive salon where you were told how to look, at an outrageous price, the conventional beauty salon for women only, and the conventional barber shop, which was limited in what it could offer. We wanted to create a unique alternative, where you could get your hair cut *exactly* as you wanted it by expert craftspeople at a modest price. That really came to one fundamental principle: to strive for perfection—the perfect haircut at an affordable price. To keep the quality up, we decided to do something no one else did—recruit people from beauty schools and give them a new pride in their craft by offering them an unprecedented opportunity to make a decent living in a 'new industry.' And to keep the price down, while maintaining quality, we had to develop remarkably efficient techniques that we could teach to our people. It was really a revolution in the industry."

After the meeting with Emmett, Rappaport managed to scrape up $1,100 in borrowed money for his half of the start-up capital. And while total investment capital of $2,200 may seem small for launching a national chain of salons, it was a fortune to a couple of lean-thinking, bootstrapping entrepreneurs. Rappaport and Emmett bought used equipment and renovated the place themselves. Recalls Rappaport, "We even bought warped lumber at giveaway prices and straightened it out ourselves. We drew on every craft skill we had developed. We painted the chairs and plastered the walls. We designed the salon and built the fixtures, even designed the Supercuts logo." Humble beginnings for an operation that now has nearly five hundred franchise outlets and grosses well over $100 million a year.

Rappaport and Emmett are particularly proud of the fact that they were able to hold the price of a haircut down to six dollars for nine years. "In 1984 we had to raise it to eight dollars," Rappaport laments. "Even with our efficiency the cost of doing business became impossible at that low figure. Eight bucks for a quality cut is still one hell of a bargain, though."

What makes the Supercuts story outstanding? It certainly has a spectacular rags-to-riches flavor. But more important is Rappaport's decision to stick with his company and continually reinvest time and money to refine it. With his corporation's monetary clout, Rappaport and his partner could easily diversify and buy into a variety of growth industries. Conventional wisdom would even say that such diversification would be the smart fiscal course to follow. "Sure, we could do any number of things with our money," Rappaport says, "but our goal is just to make our company better—better management, better marketing, improved haircutting efficiency . . . moving toward the perfect haircut. After all, we're craftsmen. And perfection is the craftsman's ultimate goal."

By this point you should have learned just about everything an SE needs to know: the attitude, the skill transfer, the thought processes, the financing strategies, the marketing strategies, and the management strategies. Think of your newfound knowledge as a grammar of sorts. You know what makes for good sentences; now you can get down to the business of creating Pulitzer Prize–winning prose.

EXERCISE 7: CREATING SPIN-OFFS

This exercise will enhance your ability to think of bold, creative spin-off projects. Think back to Chapter 2 and the ballpoint-pen exercise, then apply the same creative thinking to the following problem:

You have started a business selling imported glass ornaments. From your original investment of $2,500 you have grossed $3,500 and sold out your entire stock of ornaments. Unfortunately, after paying some pressing bills and buying groceries, you find only $1,500 in your bank account and 100 wooden shipping boxes in your basement. Your object—convert these assets into $5,000 cash for reinvestment in your next batch of glass ornaments.

You could:

1) Buy paint, turn the boxes into old-fashioned toy chests, and sell them for $50 each.

2) Turn a crate into a soapbox from which you can sing, play the harmonica, dance, or give lessons in entrepreneurship, using another crate to collect for your performance. Have your friends join you and split the profits.

3) Attach wheels to the crates and host a soapbox derby for local kids. Then raffle off the ten fastest cars.

Think of three other projects that could change each box into a $50 bill, then apply this sort of wild spin-off thinking to the project ideas you developed in Exercise 4. How could you brainstorm them into other money-making ideas? Remember, creating crazy scenarios doesn't cost a dime, but one of them might just make you a fortune.

EPILOGUE

Having imparted to his disciples all that he knew, Master Hui prepared to send Shen Ti and his companions into the world. "Before you leave," said the Master, "I wish to give each of you a gift that will serve you as you encounter the inevitable storms and dangers beyond my garden." Holding up a small flat lacquered box, he said, "Who can guess the gift?"

Cheng Wu spoke first. "Gold coins, Master Hui, which may save us from poverty?"

"No," replied the Master. "Unlike gold, which quickly disappears, this gift will last forever."

"A strong knife?" ventured Ming Su.

"No. This gift is stronger than any weapon."

Shen Ti took the box in his hand, hefted it, and said, "It must be a book that contains all your wisdom so that we may never forget what you taught us."

Master Hui smiled indulgently. "You surprise me, Shen Ti. Of all my disciples, I had expected you to guess the nature of this gift. Did you not once say that independence is the greatest gift a teacher can bestow on his students?"

As he turned the box in his hands, Shen Ti's eyes suddenly grew bright. "Then I know what it is, this one gift that will serve us forever." And with that he opened the box and gazed smilingly at his own image reflected from the mirror encased therein.

Honor yourself with a look in a mirror. If you take anything from this book to heart, adopt the philosophy embodied in Master Hui's parting gift of independence. It will serve you well as a Soft-Skilled Entrepreneur. SE's know that in the hurly-burly press of our world's complex daily affairs, it can appear that events happen *to* you, that you are at the mercy of other people's actions and of events beyond your control. But it's all a matter of perspective. If you rise above the turmoil of the Techno Age you can see how to gain full control over your destiny.

From a higher perspective you will see the path toward fulfillment of your needs and dreams. In the world of business you create your own secret formulas for success. Luck is merely a faithful follower to those who act on their dreams with confidence, commitment, calculated risk, and tenacity.

If you choose the path of the SE, you may not achieve your financial and life-style goals overnight—or at all, for that matter. But rather than growing old and wondering what *would* have happened if you had only *tried*, you will come out a winner in the most important race of all: the race for self-respect. In an age when too many people have relinquished control over their lives, yielding their fates to technocrats, specialists, consultants, corporations, and government agencies, you will take pride in having practiced the belief that individuals can still make the greatest mark of all.

SE LIBRARY

Soft-Skilled Entrepreneurs exploit every available guide they can find to make their projects succeed. This catalog offers a selection of resources ranging from the nitty-gritty of how to set up and maintain a business to suggested reading for monitoring Techno Age trends.

I. BUSINESS BOOKS AND PERIODICALS

These books and magazines cover virtually every aspect of setting up and running a small business. There is some overlap, so you might want to browse through several before deciding which ones best meet your particular needs.

General Business

Be Your Own Boss: Complete Indispensable Hands-on Guide to Starting and Running Your Own Business. Dana Shilling. Penguin, New York, 1983 (paper, $8.95). Covers basic start-up considerations: funding, employee practices and policies, taxes, paperwork, expansion, failures, and alternatives to bankruptcy.

Boardroom Reports (newsletter). Boardroom Reports, Inc., 500 Fifth Ave., New York, NY 10110. Bimonthly, $49/yr. Geared for large corporations, but lots of advice is applicable to small business owners too. Covers management techniques and tools, taxes, information sources, economic trends, and other pertinent business issues.

Building a Mail-Order Business: A Complete Manual for Success. William A. Cohen, John Wiley & Sons, New York, 1982 (cloth, $17.95). Detailed guidance for all aspects of the mail-order business. Covers setting up, financing, and marketing.

Complete Guide to Buying and Selling a Business. Arnold Goldstein. New American Library, New York, 1983 (paper, $9.95). Provides criteria for determining what a business is really worth. Also gives detailed advice, illustrated by case studies, on obtaining financing, carrying out negotiations, drawing up contracts, and dealing with legal issues.

How to Start and Manage Your Own Business. Gardiner Green. New American Library, New York, 1983 (paper, $3.95). Advice for small business people on finances, selecting professional services, management, and marketing. Provides various financial strategies and alternatives ranging from bank loans to small business investment companies.

In Business (magazine). J. G. Press, Inc., Box 323, Emmaus, PA 18049, bimonthly, $18/yr. Solid and practical information on important topics such as how to garner loans, choose an accountant, design ads, expand, sell out, and other key topics. Written in an informative and lively style.

Inside the Family Business. Leon A. Danco. Center for Family Business, The University Press, Cleveland, OH, 1980 (cloth, $19.95). Outlines the stages of a family business and the steps that should be taken at each stage to ensure continuing success. Covers issues ranging from including a spouse and employees in plans and goals, to assuring the smooth and beneficial transition of ownership of a family business upon the founder's retirement.

The National Home Business Report (newsletter). Box 2137, Naperville, IL 60566, bimonthly, $18/yr. Covers the most commonly asked questions about starting and running a business—taxes, accounting, setting up, etc. Good timely information.

Working from Home. Paul and Sarah Edwards. Tarcher, Los Angeles, 1985 (paper, $10.45). Covers management, legal, psychological, social, and other important issues. Excellent advice for the novice and the experienced home-based business person alike.

Accounting

Practical Bookkeeping of Small Business. Mary Lee Dyer. Contemporary Books, Chicago, 1976 (paper, $10.95). Excellent workbook for someone with little experience in how business finances are organized. Covers key aspects of bookkeeping, accounting, payroll, and other basic functions.

The Professional Report (newsletter). TPR Publishing, Inc. 81 Montgomery St., Scarsdale, NY 10583, monthly, $48/yr. Technical tax and management advice. Includes updates on recent IRS cases.

Management

How to Save Your Business. Arnold Goldstein. Enterprise Publishing, Wilmington, DE, 1983 (cloth, $24.95). A comprehensive guide to avoiding bankruptcy. Gives good strategies for reshaping a financially troubled company, staving off creditors, and staying afloat in turbulent waters.

How to Start, Run, and Stay in Business. Gregory F. Kishel and Patricia Gunter Kishel. John Wiley & Sons, New York, 1981 (paper, $8.95). Interactive guide structured to help small business people make crucial day-to-day decisions that spell the difference between success and failure. Offers advice from choosing the form of ownership and securing financing, through hiring, inventory, record-keeping, pricing, and advertising.

Small Business Survival Guide. Bob Coleman. W. W. Norton, New York, 1984 (cloth, $18.95). Examination of the most common pitfalls and ways to avoid them. Appendices on reading business statements, offers to purchase, etc.

Finance

Starting on a Shoestring. Arnold Goldstein. John Wiley & Sons, New York, 1984 (paper, $12.95). A truly SE approach to starting a business without a bankroll. Gives numerous techniques and examples for getting the most out of every dollar. Good solid advice for the novice and pro alike.

Start-Up Money: How to Finance Your New Small Business. Mike P. McKeever. Nolo Press, Berkeley, CA, 1984 (paper, $17.95). A complete look at conventional financing methods, including how to start with a concise business plan/loan package and end up with a successful business. Stresses the plan-writing process as an opportunity to hone an idea, not simply to document one.

Legal

The Complete Legal Guide for Your Small Business. Paul Adams. John Wiley & Sons, New York, 1982 (cloth, $21.95). Guidance for preparing legal documents for day-to-day commercial transactions. Demystifies legal forms, paragraph by paragraph.

How to Proceed in Business Legally: The Entrepreneur's Preventive Law Guide (Federal edition). Stanley G. Jackson. Prentice-Hall, Englewood Cliffs, NJ, 1984 (paper, $12.95). Explains in broad terms the federal regulations concerning small businesses. Invaluable information on topics such as incorporation laws, taxation, stock, and other basic business issues. It also describes unfair business and trade practices that could be deemed illegal.

Incorporating: A Guide for Small Business Owners. Carolyn M. Vella and John J. McGonagle. American Management Association, New York, 1984 (paper, $15.95). A very thorough guide that lays out both the pros and cons and the how-to's of incorporation for the small business owner. Includes insightful pre- and post-incorporation checklists as well as a final section on dissolving an ineffective corporation.

How to Protect and Benefit from Your Ideas. American Patent Law Association, Inc., Suite 203, 2001 Jefferson Davis Highway, Arlington, VA 22202 ($10). Explains what idea protection is all about, and covers topics such as common pitfalls, disclosure, getting marketing and legal help, and making money from an idea. Written in nonlegalese. An excellent reference source for the inventive entrepreneur.

To request copyright forms, write to the Copyright Office, Library of Congress, Washington, DC 20559. Form TX is used for most nondramatic works, including: fiction, nonfiction, poetry, textbooks, directories, advertising copy, reference works, and computer programs. Form PA is used for the performing arts, and Form VA is used for the visual arts. The applications for trademarks and patents are available from the Commissioner of Patents and Trademarks, Washington, DC 20231; however, they are complex and should be filled out by an attorney *who specializes in those areas.*

Forms Books

The Basic Book of Business Agreements. Arnold Goldstein. Enterprise Publishing, Inc. Wilmington, DE, 1982 (paper, $49.95). A basic book of forms and agreements covering most routine business transactions. (A companion set of forms, *The Complete Credit Collection System*, provides a similar set of forms for helping you to get paid. Also $49.95.)

How to Form Your Own Corporation Without a Lawyer for Under $50. Ted Nicholas. Enterprise Publishing, Wilmington, DE, 1985 (paper, $19.95). Gives basic forms agreements for incorporation. Specifics may vary from state to state.

The Complete Business Planner. Business Planning Institute, 270

Boylston St., Brookline, MA 02140, 1983 (paper, $49.95). A do-it-yourself kit for constructing a business plan. Covers product evaluation, marketing, competition, organization, financing, and other elements that go into a business plan.

II. CONSULTING

Consultant's Kit: Establishing and Operating Your Successful Consulting Business. Dr. Jeffrey A. Lant. JLA Publications, Cambridge, MA, 1981 (paper, $30). A complete how-to guide for starting a consulting practice. Excellent advice on focusing your thinking, networking, marketing, negotiating contracts and other business issues. Pricey, but worth it. (See follow-up work in Section III.)

Consulting Opportunities Journal. J. Stephen Lanning, P.O. Box 17674, Washington, DC 20041, bimonthly, $39/yr. Information about how to be a successful consultant. Covers networking and marketing strategies. Also includes information about professional seminars and conferences.

How to Succeed as an Independent Consultant. H. Holtz. John Wiley & Sons, New York, 1984 (cloth, $19.95). Information on marketing your skills as an independent consultant. How to establish a practice, identify the best prospects, turn prospects into hard sales leads, and turn leads into clients.

Successful Freelancing. Marion Faux. St. Martin's Press, New York, 1982 (paper, $8.95). Discusses pros and cons of free-lancing and working in the home. Covers setting up an office, financial planning, partnership vs. corporation, the IRS, selling yourself, billing, and expansion. Provides general rules, guidelines, and examples.

III. MARKETING BOOKS AND REFERENCES

Guerrilla Marketing: Secrets for Making Big Profits from Your Small Business. Jay Conrad Levinson. Houghton Mifflin, Boston, 1984 (cloth, $14.95). A true SE guide. Shows how to get maxi-ad benefits with a mini-budget. Various techniques for print, radio, and television spots. Has a retail orientation, but ideas and spirit can be translated to any kind of enterprise.

The Unabashed Self-Promoter's Guide. Dr. Jeffrey L. Lant. JLA Publications, Cambridge, MA, 1983 (paper, $30). A master collection of practical insights, tips, and methods for getting yourself known to the world. Style is elitist, price tag is high. But uniqueness and quality of the information make it well worth coughing up the money.

A number of key marketing reference sources are published by Standard Rates and Data Service (SRDS), Inc., 3004 Glenview Rd., Wilmette, IL 60091 (tel.: 312-256-6067). You can usually find them in your local library. The SRDS "family" contains the following members:

Business Publication Rates and Data. Lists rates, specifications, and contacts for U.S. and international business publications, including trade magazines. Publications are listed alphabetically and by industrial classification. Also lists publications that have specific geographic and/or demographic editions ($216/yr., monthly).

Canadian Advertising Rates and Data. Lists advertising rates for all Canadian media (publications, radio, and TV) ($157/yr., monthly).

Community Newspapers and Shopping Guides. Lists advertising rates for weekly newspapers and shopping guides ($30/yr., biannually; $18/single).

Consumer Magazines and Agri-Media Rates and Data. Advertising rates for over 1,500 consumer magazines and farm publications. Listed by consumer group ($190/yr., monthly).

Cooperative Advertising Source Directory. Lists 3,500 manufacturers who offer cooperative advertising ($132/yr., biannually; $99/single).

Direct Mail Lists Data. Lists 55,000 companies with mailing lists for sale. Grouped according to various subjects (computers, health, etc.) ($155/yr., bimonthly; $64/single issue).

Newspaper Rates and Data. Lists advertising rates for over 1,600 newspapers and newspaper groups, organized geographically ($194/yr., monthly; $93/single issue).

Print Media Production Data. Gives detailed specifications for advertising in consumer and trade magazines ($112/yr., quarterly).

Spot Radio Rates and Data. Lists advertising rates for 7,500 radio stations in market areas greater than 25,000 ($174/yr., monthly; $84/single issue).

Spot Radio—Small Markets Edition. Lists advertising data for radio stations with markets of less than 25,000 ($59/yr., biannually; $34/single).

Spot TV Rates. Lists advertising rates for virtually all TV stations in the U.S. ($157/yr., biannually; $76/single issue).

IV. MISCELLANEOUS REFERENCES

The following resources can be very helpful when you're researching a product, a market, or trying to build a network. You should be able to find them in any good business library.

Business Information Sources (rev. ed.). Lorna Daniels. University of California Press, Berkeley, CA, 1985 (cloth, $28.95). A comprehensive, annotated directory of hundreds of reference books, directories, indexes, abstracts, and other information sources. Broken down by functional business categories. Extremely useful for many aspects of running a business and developing marketing sources. Well worth owning.

The Insider's Guide to Small Business Resources. David Gumpert and Jeffrey A. Timmons. Doubleday, Garden City, NY, 1982 (cloth, $24.95). Oriented toward enabling entrepreneurs to examine business options and thereby improve the success of ventures. Information is grouped by subject (e.g., Consultants and Management Assistance, Assistance for Minority Business, Venture Capital), with overviews of the topic, lists and descriptions of contacts, descriptions of common misconceptions, and how to best understand and use sources.

Literary Market Place (LMP). R. R. Bowker Company, New York (annual editions, paper, $45). Covers the American book-publishing industry. Lists names, addresses, and editors of publishers. Organized alphabetically, geographically, and by subject. Also lists literary agents, publishing associations, consultants, and various services. A useful source for anyone planning a project related to the publishing industry.

The Information Broker's Handbook: How to Profit from the Information Age. John Everett and Elizabeth Powell Crowe. Ferret Press, 4121 Buckthorn Court, Lewisville, TX 1984, 75020, (cloth, $24.95). Explains how to organize a computerized research business. A thorough development of the subject, including topics ranging from defining what type of research you want to do, to creating your own brochure, calculating fees, legal considerations, and marketing strategies. Contains annotated list of professional research systems, magazines, books, and professional associations related to the information industry.

The Encyclopedia of Associations. Gale Research Company, Detroit, MI (biennial, three volumes). A compilation of national associations organized by subject area (e.g., business, agriculture, educational). Each listing includes name, address, telephone, size of membership, a description of activities, publications, and scope. An invaluable networking and marketing resource.

The Newsletter Yearbook Directory. The Newsletter Clearinghouse, 44 West Market St., Box 311, Rhinebeck, NY 12572 ($45). Updated annually. Lists hundreds of newsletters in various fields. Each entry provides address and phone number of publisher, name of editor, cost, frequency, date started, and other information, such as whether the newsletter seeks press releases and whether it is available in electronic form. Not the definitive one-stop source, but a useful place to begin tracking down competing newsletters or free media outlets in a field of interest to you.

The States and Small Businesses: Programs and Activities. United States Small Business Administration, 1441 L St., N.W., Washington, DC 20416. Lists government support agencies, publications, resource procurement, assistance and information centers, legislative committees, and pertinent legislation. Includes economic data and statistical tables. Organized by state.

United States Industrial Outlook: Prospects for Over 300 Industries. US Department of Commerce. Government Printing Office, Washington, DC 20014 ($15). Annual compendium of government statistics and forecasts in fifty-two industrial groupings, including computers, electronics, and various service industries. Each grouping includes current statistical profiles, trends and projection tables, and trade data for each industry. Also included are short-term and long-term prospects for each industry.

V. BOOKS ON CREATIVE THINKING

A Whack on the Side of the Head: How to Unlock Your Mind for Innovation. Roger von Oech, Ph.D. Warner Books, New York, 1983 (paper, $9.95). A fun and useful collection of techniques for enhancing your creative thinking process. Organized around opening ten "mental locks." Good exercises for SE's and others who depend on their creativity.

Conceptual Blockbusting: A Guide to Better Ideas. James L. Adams. Norton, New York, 1979 (paper, $5.95). A solid approach to creative problem-solving. Numerous games and exercises help you learn to think more productively by breaking through conceptual blocks.

VI. BOOKS ON STRESS REDUCTION

Stressmap: Finding Your Pressure Points. C. Michele Haney and Edmond W. Boenisch. Impact Publishers, San Luis Obispo, CA,

1982 (paper, $5.95). An imaginative set of action-oriented self-tests, checklists, exercises, and meditations. Easy reading and good relief for Techno Age stresses.

Life After Stress. Martin Shaffer. Contemporary Books, Chicago, 1983 (paper, $8.95). Solid work that covers signs of stress, principles of stress reduction, and discussions of stress in the work and home environments. Good exercises.

Coping with Difficult People. Robert M. Bramson, Ph.D. Ballantine, New York, 1981 (paper, $2.95). Describes how to deal with six species of difficult people (hostiles/aggressives, complainers, silents/unresponsives, superagreeables, negativists, and know-it-alls). Even if such characters don't cause you stress, you'll find the book useful in your daily business interactions and negotiations.

The Stress Relief Kit. Robin Casarjian and Naomi Raiselle. Soundiscoveries, Inc., Box 194, Boston, MA 02117 ($25). Kit contains two cassettes designed to help create the calm, peaceful atmosphere necessary to reduce stress. "Daily Life" recording establishes distance from stressful situations while directing the focus to the cause of the stress. Nine-minute "Relaxing" tape can be used anytime to recapture that distance and clear away anxiety. Good tools for learning to cope with stressful business situations. Soundiscoveries also offers a ninety-day self-help program, "The Stress Reducer" ($69), which includes six tapes and workbook.

VII. ASSOCIATIONS AND ORGANIZATIONS

An association can be a tremendous boost to an entrepreneur in terms of services, technical assistance, and network-building opportunities. At the very least, they may be the only outlet through which you can get group health insurance.

General Business Associations

International Council for Small Business. Brooks Hall, University of Georgia, Athens, GA 30602 (tel.: 404-542-5760). Dues:

$10–$95/yr. An umbrella organization that brings together academics, government officials, small business persons, and representatives from other business organizations. Sponsors conferences and publishes the *Journal of Small Business Management*. Developing a Minority Business Division to better serve blacks and Hispanics.

National Small Business Association. NSB Building, 1604 K Street, N.W., Washington, DC 20006 (tel.: 202-293-8830). Dues: $75 and up. Primarily lobbies to promote what its members perceive to be legislation favorable to small businesses. Offers group disability, hospital, life, and accident insurance, as well as a retirement plan. Publishes *The Voice of Small Business*, which keeps track of laws and regulations affecting small businesses.

Small Business Service Bureau Inc. 544 Main St., Box 1441, Worcester, MA 01601 (tel.: 617-756-3513; in MA 800-262-2981; outside MA 800-343-0939). Dues: $50–$75/yr. Lobbies nationally for small businesses. Offers health (including HMO) insurance, computer discounts, and management assistance (including a toll-free consulting service). Publishes the *Bulletin*, which reports on legislation and gives management advice for small businesses.

Associations for Women in Business

American Business Women's Association. 9100 Ward Parkway, P.O. Box 8728, Kansas City, MO 64114 (tel.: 816-361-6621). Dues: $18/yr.; one-time initial fee, $38.50. Serves to enhance the educational and professional advancement of women. Offers prescription and travel discounts as well as medical and life insurance. Special vehicle accident insurance is included in membership. Publishes *Women in Business*. Also awards scholarships to students and businesswomen.

American Society of Professional and Executive Women. 1511 Walnut St., Philadelphia, PA 19102 (tel.: 215-563-4415). Dues: $42/yr. Founded to help promote positive attitudes in women in business. Conducts seminars, provides discount book service and travel and dining discounts. Offers life-insurance program. Publishes *Successful Woman*, which focuses on the politics of power and self-motivation.

National Alliance of Home-based Businesswomen. P.O. Box 306, Midland Park, NJ 07432. Dues: $30/yr., prorated after July of May–April membership year. Dedicated to solving home-based business problems: isolation, lack of credibility, and professional image. NAHB offers a life-insurance package, access to corporate rates on business-magazine subscriptions, car rentals, and hotel-chain accommodations. Associate membership available even if you haven't started your business yet. Publishes quarterly newsletter, *Alliance*, which discusses legislative issues and promotes networking among members.

National Association of Women Business Owners. 645 N. Michigan Ave., Chicago, IL 60611 (tel.: 312-661-1700). Dues: $60/yr. (registration fee: $20). An affiliate of the World Association of Women Entrepreneurs. Mainly a networking organization, it is gaining political clout through its work with Congress and the SBA. Publishes a newsletter, *Statement*, which primarily reports on organizational activities.

Associations for Communicators

American Medical Writers Association (AMWA). 5272 River Rd., Suite 410, Bethesda, MD 20816 (tel.: 301-986-9119). Dues: $55/yr. The only professional society devoted exclusively to the improvement of communications in medicine and allied health fields. Provides educational workshops and seminars for members. Also provides excellent networking opportunities. Regional chapters throughout United States and Canada. Publishes bimonthly newsletter and quarterly journal *(Medical Communications)*. Free-lance membership directory published every eighteen months.

Society for Technical Communication (STC). 815 15th St., N.W., Washington, DC 20005 (tel.: 202-737-0035). Dues: $50/yr. (Initiation fee.) Regional chapters meet periodically to discuss various aspects of technical communication. Good networking possibilities. Quarterly journal: *Technical Communications*.

National Writers Club. 1450 South Havana, Suite 620, Aurora, CO 80012 (tel.: 303-751-7844). Dues: $40/$50 year. An information and networking organization for writers. Provides legal and marketing information through its consulting services, workshops, and publications. Offers group life, medical, and disability insurance, and a group savings plan.

VIII. FUNDING

Venture Capital

Guide to Venture Capital Sources. S. Pratt and J. Morris. Capital Publishing Corp., Wellesley Hills, MA, 1983. Collection of articles by various authors on such matters as overviews of the venture-capital industry and entrepreneurship, sources of financing, how to raise capital, and when to go public. Includes a directory of U.S. and Canadian venture-capital companies, with location, contacts, and financing stipulations.

Government

Many kinds of help are available from the U.S. Small Business Administration (SBA), which has a variety of loan, educational, and technical-assistance programs. There are more than 100 SBA offices throughout the country. Some SBA loan programs work in conjunction with regular business loans obtained through banks and other lending institutions. Under the programs, the SBA guarantees up to 90 percent of the amount of these loans. Other special loan programs aid local development companies, provide seasonal loans to seasonal businesses, energy loans, disaster assistance, and loans for physically handicapped owners. For general information, contact:

Small Business Administration
Washington, DC 20416
Tel.: 202-655-4000

The SBA loan programs of most interest to budding entrepreneurs are offered through hundreds of SBIC's (Small Business Investment Companies). Each SBIC is a privately owned and operated firm that provides equity capital and long-term loans to small businesses. For more information about SBIC's and a directory of local centers, call or write:

National Association of Small Business Investment
    Companies
618 Washington Bldg.
Washington, DC 20005
Tel.: 202-833-8230

In addition to SBIC's, funds can sometimes be obtained through a MESBIC—a Minority Enterprise Small Business Investment Company (a MESBIC is now officially called a "301(d) SBIC"). MESBIC's are authorized solely to assist firms owned by socially or economically disadvantaged persons. Complete information and a directory of local MESBIC's can be obtained through:

American Association of Minority Enterprise Small
    Business Investment Companies
915 15th St., N.W., Suite 700
Washington, DC 20005
Tel.: 202-347-8600

In addition to MESBIC's, the SBA also sponsors more than 100 Minority Business Development Centers (MBDC's), which provide technical, management, and marketing assistance especially for minorities. For information about the Minority Business Development Agency, contact:

MBDA Information Clearinghouse
Minority Business Development Agency
U.S. Department of Commerce
14th & Constitution Avenue, N.W.
Washington, DC 20230
Tel.: 202-377-2414

Special assistance programs for women and veterans are also

operated through local SBA offices. Check your phone book under "U.S. Government."

Two other useful government funding guides are:

How to Finance Your Small Business with Government Money: SBA Loans. R. Hayes and J. Howell. CBI Publishing Co., Boston, 1980. In-depth guide to SBA loan application process, including: eligibility, preparing proposals, financial calculations, and procurement assistance, with detailed descriptions and formulas of financial statement preparation. Appendices include a glossary, sample business plan, and loan proposal. Slightly dated, but the basic formats are good.

Small Business Guide to Federal R & D Funding Opportunities. Human Sciences Research, Westgate Research Park, McLean, VA 22102, 1983. Overview of information on basic grants and funding, a "venture-capital primer," government sources of technical information, and descriptions of various government agency activities and contacts. Emphasis is on research and technology rather than general business.

IX. CULTURAL MEDIA MENU

As mentioned in Chapter 4, information is the lifeblood of the Soft-Skilled Entrepreneur. The key to coming up with new ideas and keeping your old ones from becoming stale is to scan as many sources as you can. In addition to your basic newsmagazines, *The Wall Street Journal*, and at least two major daily newspapers (preferably one from each coast), a selection of the following information sources will keep you well abreast of Techno Age currents:

American Health. American Health Partners, 80 Fifth Ave., New York, NY 10011. Monthly, $23/yr. Excellent means for keeping up with health and fitness trends. Covers medicine, nutrition, exercise, diet, and other aspects of health science. Well written and extremely informative.

Black Enterprise. Earl G. Graves Publishing Company, 130 Fifth Ave., New York, NY 10011. Monthly, $15/yr. Contains profiles of black entrepreneurs and business owners as well as feature articles on such topics as personal finance and tax reform. Covers entire range from small businesses to large corporations.

BusinessWeek. McGraw-Hill, Inc., 1221 Avenue of the Americas, New York, NY 10020. Weekly, $39.95/yr. National and international developments in business and finance. Broken down by various aspects of finance, management, and general business news. Good for scanning all trend areas.

Whole Earth Review. Point, 27 Gate 5 Rd., Sausalito, CA 94966, quarterly, $18/yr. This is published by the people who brought us *The Whole Earth Catalog*. In addition to entertaining stories and tidbits about books, services, and gadgets that you never hear of anywhere else, this is a good way of keeping tabs on what's happening in terms of alternative economics, technologies, and cultural practices.

Entrepreneur. Chase Revel, Inc., 2311 Pontius Ave., Los Angeles, CA 90064. Monthly, $24.50/yr. Profiles of entrepreneurs, with emphasis on how they achieve success. Focuses on unusual businesses and trends.

Forbes. Forbes, Inc., 60 Fifth Ave., New York, NY 10011. Biweekly, $39/yr. News for and about large corporations and their executives. Good for keeping up with general trends as seen from the perspectives of the big guys.

Fortune. Time Inc., Time & Life Bldg., Rockefeller Center, New York, N.Y. 10020, biweekly, $39/yr. National news and trends in business and finance. Emphasis same as *Forbes*. Good for general scanning.

The Futurist. World Future Society, 4916 St. Elmo Avenue, Bethesda, MD 20814, bimonthly, $20/yr. Articles deal with options and directions of change for the future. Subjects range from education and leisure trends to shifting job patterns and "geoeconomics." Thorough, well researched, and well worth a subscription. The WFS also publishes many forward-looking books on important issues related to social and economic change as well as a concise monthly abstract of books, articles, and reports concerning future trends.

Inc. Inc. Publishing Corporation, P.O. Box 2538, Boulder, CO 80322. Monthly, $24/yr. Focuses on rapidly growing companies. Includes advice on finance, marketing, and management. Tends to focus on fast-lane high-tech companies and their executives, with a "how-they-did-it" bent. Good for keeping abreast of innovative business thinking.

InfoWorld. Popular Computing, Inc., 375 Cochituate Road, Framingham, MA 01701. Weekly, $31/yr. Of the scores of computer publications, *InfoWorld* has the most useful overviews of the industry and how it affects the rest of the world. It also has the unusual aspect of being consistently well-written. If you want to keep up with computers, and want to scan only one magazine, this is the one.

John Naisbitt's Trend Letter. The Naisbitt Group, 1101 30th St., N.W., Washington, DC 20007. Biweekly, $98/yr. Expensive, but devoted solely to trends, and useful to entrepreneurs. Topics covered include: business economics, human relations, financial institutions, information, the global economy, computers, transportation, rising industries, law and justice, high-tech industries, agriculture, housing and real estate, energy, employment, the environment, women's movement, education, government, health, arts and entertainment, and several miscellaneous categories.

Nation's Business. Chamber of Commerce of the United States, 1615 H St., N.W., Washington, DC 20062. Monthly, $22/yr. Follows business developments from the Chamber of Commerce point of view. Lots of information and advice for the small business person. Good for general business trends.

New Product Development. Point Publishing Co., Inc., P.O. Box 1309, Point Pleasant, NJ 08742. Monthly, $75/yr. Describes new markets and products. Features articles on marketing of new products and projected market growth areas. Briefly discusses some of the latest products from R&D labs. Includes reviews of new product and management books.

Savvy. Savvy Company, P.O. Box 2495, Boulder, CO 80321. Monthly, $12/yr. Geared to the woman executive but has useful information for SE's. A wealth of networking information in feature articles. "Frontlines" focuses on women business innovators. Management-strategy articles helpful to anyone who manages people.

Success. Success Magazine Company, P.O. Box 3038, Harlan, IA 51537. Monthly, $17.95/yr. Flashy articles focus on how people achieve success and how others can be successful too. Focuses on mind-set and strategies. Follows new trends in business styles and management.

Working Woman. Hal Publications, 342 Madison Ave., New York, NY 10173. Monthly, $18/yr. Strong on financial and business tips, from how to manage your money to how to manage your staff. Directed toward women middle-managers. "Enterprise" and "Business Watch" sections are especially useful to entrepreneurs looking for new ideas.

Venture. Venture Magazine, Inc., 521 Fifth Ave., New York, NY 10175. Monthly, $18/yr. Talks about new business trends and entrepreneurial opportunities. Lots of practical information and advice, including how to obtain venture capital and develop a business strategy. Instructive profiles of successful entrepreneurs. One of the most useful publications devoted solely to entrepreneurism.

Science and Technology. The Research Institute of America, 589 Fifth Ave., New York, NY 10017. Monthly, $36/yr. Discusses new technologies emerging in a variety of fields, such as biotechnology, robotics, and computers. Summarizes state-of-the-art developments and predicts their impact on the marketplace.

Science News. 231 West Center St., Marion, OH 43306. Weekly, $27.50/yr. Good summaries of articles in major scientific magazines and journals. Not always cutting edge, but generally useful if you don't have time to scan lots of publications.

X. ELECTRONIC DATA BASES

If you have a computer and a modem (which allows computers to talk with other computers via the phone lines), you can tap into a number of "electric libraries" or data banks to: 1) find specific information or 2) read abstracts or sections of publications that would otherwise be too time-consuming to track down or too expensive to subscribe to. While electronic searching can be very costly, used wisely it can easily pay for itself in terms of ideas you develop from expanding your information sources. If you're thinking of using electronic data bases, you might first take a look at *Inc.* magazine's *Databasics* by Doran Howitt and Marvin I. Weinberger (Garland Publishing Inc., paper, $16.95), which includes concise and nontechnical explanations of how to conduct electronic information searches, and which data bases are best suited to your needs. The following three data banks are especially useful for entrepreneurs and small business owners:

Dialog (3460 Hillview Ave., Palo Alto, CA 94304, 800-227-1927, in California 800-982-5838). This is probably the best known of all the major data banks and consists of some 200 individual data bases. The data bases cover topics ranging from art history to zoology, and can cost anywhere from $25/hr. to $100/hr. plus the telephone charges. An average cost is between $5 and $20. (There is no initial fee or monthly charge, but the manual is $50.) Dialog is difficult to use without training, and the company suggests you take one of their $145 courses. Another alternative is a program called In Search, which allows you to peruse the data bases in plain English and pick up what you need (available from Menlo Corporation, 4633 Old Ironsides, Suite 400, Santa Clara, CA 95050, 408-986-1200).

Knowledge Index (3460 Hillview Ave., Palo Alto, CA 94304, 800-227-5510, in California 415-858-3796). This is a condensed version of Dialog, and contains twenty-five representative data bases. It is available from six P.M. to five A.M. during the week (more hours available on weekends) and is substantially less money (a flat $24/hr. including telecommunications charges). There is a $35 registration fee, which includes the user manual. Knowledge Index data bases can quickly and inexpensively provide a wealth of marketing information and background for an idea you want to develop or evaluate. The Business, Magazine, and News data bases are particularly valuable to entrepreneurs.

NewsNet (945 Haverford Road, Bryn Mawr, PA 19010, 800-345-1301, in Pennsylvania 215-527-8030). NewsNet is an unusual data base that has some 250 specialty newsletters in their entirety. You can read or scan current issues, or dig through back issues. The charge for using NewsNet ranges from $18 to $48 per hour with a $15 monthly subscription fee. Given the fact that some of the newsletters would cost two, three, even four hundred dollars to subscribe to individually, this is an extremely cost-effective way of gaining access to valuable information. One interesting feature of NewsNet is its electronic "clipping" service, called NewsFlash. You tell the data base the key words you're looking for, and the system will flag any articles that meet your criteria.

If you decide to read newsletters on NewsNet, the following are most useful for tracking Techno Age trends:

Cable Hotline. Local and national news and trends in the cable programming industry.

FTC FOIA Log. A weekly listing of Freedom of Information Act requests received by the FTC. (Interesting way to find potential competitors.)

Federal Grants and Contracts Weekly. Lists grant and contract opportunities in research, training, and services.

Hi-Tech Contracts Weekly. Lists federal grant and contract opportunities for small research firms.

Invention Management. Provides insight into new trends in technology development, protection, and commercialization. Covers such areas as R&D management and financing, licensing and acquisition, and copyright and trade-secret developments.

Patent Newsletter. Week-by-week information on new patents, including abstracts, drawings, and ownership data. There are specific newsletters for eight technology areas, such as telecommunications, robotics, and packaging.

Micro Moonlighter. Describes numerous ways to make money on the side if you own a computer. Also has articles with tips and suggestions by people who successfully moonlight with their micros.

Seybold Report on Professional Computers. Detailed information about professional computer hardware and software. Includes evaluations, trends, and convention reports.

Update/The American States. Provides economic, social, legal, and marketing data and trends for each of the states and for the country as a whole.

Videonews. Information about the latest developments in the video industry and their impact on the marketplace.

INDEX

ABOUT THE AUTHOR

Author, free-lance scholar, and entrepreneur Steven J. Bennett has refined the art of playing hardball with soft skills. Since receiving a Master's Degree in East Asian Studies from Harvard University, where he studied the ancient Chinese science of house and tomb placement, he has worked for a diverse range of private and public concerns as a writer, editor, research coordinator, and marketing consultant. Today he is president of S. J. Bennett & Company, Inc., a thriving media firm in Cambridge, MA that specializes in high-tech communications, and executive director of the Bennett Information Group, a complete book and idea development service.